Wayland Mass.

The Town of Wayland in the Civil War of 1861-1865

As Represented in the Army and Navy of the American Union

Wayland Mass.

The Town of Wayland in the Civil War of 1861-1865
As Represented in the Army and Navy of the American Union

ISBN/EAN: 9783337125332

Printed in Europe, USA, Canada, Australia, Japan

Cover: Foto ©ninafisch / pixelio.de

SERIES D.

MISCELLANEOUS.

A

HISTORY OF ENGLISH SOUNDS

FROM THE EARLIEST PERIOD,

INCLUDING AN

INVESTIGATION OF THE GENERAL LAWS OF SOUND CHANGE, AND FULL WORD LISTS.

BY

HENRY SWEET, ESQ.,

MEMBER OF COUNCIL OF THE PHILOLOGICAL AND EARLY ENGLISH TEXT SOCIETIES,
EDITOR OF THE OLD ENGLISH VERSION OF GREGORY'S CURA PASTORALIS.

(*From the Transactions of the Philological Society for* 1873-4.)

LONDON:
PUBLISHED FOR THE ENGLISH DIALECT SOCIETY
BY TRÜBNER & CO., 57 AND 59, LUDGATE HILL.

MDCCCLXXIV.

CONTENTS.

PREFACE.

ADDRESSED TO MEMBERS OF THE ENGLISH DIALECT SOCIETY.

THE History of English Sounds, by Mr. Henry Sweet, was originally written for the London Philological Society, in further illustration of the great work on Early English Pronunciation by Mr. Alexander J. Ellis. Upon application to the Council of the Philological Society, and to the author, permission was at once obtained for making arrangements whereby additional copies of the work should be struck off for the use of members of the English Dialect Society. The importance of it to all who study English sounds, especially such sounds as are frequently well preserved in some of our provincial dialects, will soon become apparent to the careful reader. But as there may be some amongst our members who may not be aware of what has been lately achieved in the study of phonetics, a few words of introduction may not be out of place here.

I have more than once received letters from correspondents who boldly assert that, of some of our dialectal sounds, no representation is possible, and that it is useless to attempt it. Against such a sweeping denunciation of the study of phonetics it would be vain to argue. It may be sufficient merely to remark that precisely the same argument of "impossibility" was used, not so many years ago, against the introduction of the use of steam locomotives upon railways. The opinions of such as are unable to imagine how things which they cannot do themselves may, nevertheless, be achieved by others, will not be much regarded by such as desire progress and improvement.

It may, however, be conceded that no system of symbols existed which was of sufficient scientific accuracy until the publication of Mr. Melville Bell's singular and wonderful volume entitled—"Visible Speech: the Science of Universal Alphabetics: or Self-Interpreting Physiological Letters for the Printing and Writing of all Languages in one Alphabet; elucidated by Theoretical Explanations, Tables, Diagrams, and Examples." Now in this system none of the usual alphabetical characters appear at all, nor is the alphabet founded upon any one language. It is a wholly new collection of symbols, adapted for all or most of the sounds which the human voice is capable of producing, and is founded upon the most strictly scientific principles, each symbol being so chosen as to define the disposition of the organs used in producing the sound which the symbol is intended to represent. How this wonderful result has been achieved, the reader may easily discover for himself, either by consulting that work, or another by the same author which every one interested in the study of phonetics is earnestly recommended to procure, at the cost of only *one shilling*. The title of this latter work, consisting of only sixteen pages in quarto, is:—English Visible Speech for the Million, etc.; by Alex. Melville Bell. London: Simpkin, Marshall & Co.; London and New York: Trübner & Co. A fair and candid examination of this pamphlet will shew the reader, better than any detailed description can do, how the study of sounds has been rendered possible. Every work on phonetics will, no doubt, always be based upon, or have reference to, Mr. Bell's system, and therefore it is the more important that, at the very least, the existence of it should be widely known.

The work of Mr. Ellis is entitled:—On Early English Pronunciation, with especial reference to Shakspere and Chaucer, by Alexander J. Ellis, F.R.S. The first two parts were published in 1869 by three societies in combination, viz. the Philological Society, the Early English Text Society, and the Chaucer Society; and the third part, by the same societies, in 1870. The work is not yet completed, and the fourth part, not yet published, will contain a full account of our modern English provincial dialects, shewing their distribution and connections. Mr. Ellis employs a system of symbols called *palæotype*, but, as every one of these has its exact equivalent in Mr. Bell's system, it admits of the same degree of accuracy, and has the advantage of being wholly represented by ordinary printing-types.

The next system is that invented by Mr. Ellis for the *special* representation of English dialectal sounds, and denominated *Glossic*.[1] By the kindness of the author, a copy of the tract upon Glossic is in the hands of every member of our Society. The attention of readers is directed to page 11 of that tract, where the thirty-six vowels of Mr. Bell's Visible Speech have their equivalent values in Glossic properly tabulated.

In Mr. Sweet's volume, now in the reader's hands, the corresponding table of vowel-sounds is given at page 5, and one principal object of this short Preface is to shew how Mr. Sweet's symbols and the 'Glossic' symbols agree together, and how, again, each table agrees with that of Mr. Bell.

I shall refer, then, to the three tables as given at p. 5 of Mr. Sweet's book, at p. 11 of the Glossic tract, and at p. 8 of Visible Speech for the Million. See also p. 14 of Mr. Ellis's Early English Pronunciation.

[1] The system called *Glossotype*, illustrated at p. 16 of Mr. Ellis's Early English Pronunciation, may be considered as now *cancelled*, and superseded by *Glossic*.

Mr. Ellis and Mr. Sweet agree with Mr. Bell in their use of the terms *High*, *Mid*, and *Low;* in their use of the terms *Back*, *Mixed*, and *Front;* and in their use of the terms *Wide* and *Wide-round*. The only difference is that Mr. Sweet uses the term *Narrow* instead of *Primary* (see page 4, note 1), and also uses the more exact term *Narrow-round* in place of what Mr. Ellis calls *Round* simply. As Mr. Sweet has *numbered* his sounds, it is easy to tabulate the correspondence of the systems in the following manner. I denote here Mr. Sweet's sounds by the *number* only, and include the Glossic symbol within square brackets, in the usual manner.

1. [uu'].	4. [ea].	7. [EE].	10. [U'].	13. [I'].	16. [I].
2. [UU].	5. [U].	8. [AI].	11. [AA].	14. [Λ'].	17. [E].
3. [ua].	6. [ua'].	9. [AE].	12. [AH].	15. [E'].	18. [A].
19. [oo].	22. [ui'].	25. [ui].	28. [uo].	31. [uo'].	34. [UE].
20. [OA].	23. [oa'].	26. [EO].	29. [ΔO].	32. [ao'].	35. [OE].
21. [AU].	24. [au'].	27. [eo'].	30. [o].	33. [o'].	36. [oe'].

Now it should be clearly understood that these two systems are both perfectly exact, because both refer to the same positions of the organs of voice; but, as soon as these sounds come to be described by illustrative examples, a few slight apparent discrepancies arise, solely from a difference of individual pronunciation, even in the case of common 'key-words.' I believe I am correct in saying that even Mr. Bell's 'key-words' do not represent to everybody the exact sounds intended, but are better understood by a North-country man than by a resident in London. Mr. Ellis describes this difficulty in the following words: "At the latter end of his treatise Mr. Melville Bell has given in to the practice of key-words, and assigned them to his symbols. Let the reader be careful not to take the value of his symbol from his own pronunciation of the key-words, or from any other person's. Let him first determine the value of the symbol from the exact description and diagram of the speech-organs,—or if possible also from the living voice of some one thoroughly acquainted with the system—and then determine Mr. Bell's own pronunciation of the key-word from the known value of the symbol. This pronunciation in many instances differs from that which I am accustomed to give it, especially in foreign words."

In order to steer clear of such minor difficulties, Mr. Sweet has adopted a very simple system of notation, which only aims at representing the broader distinctions between vowels, using, for example, the same symbol [a] for the mid-back-wide and the low-back-wide sounds (nos. 11 and 12), without further distinction, and defining it only as the sound *a*, as most commonly heard in the word *father*. Roughly speaking, then, the symbols which Mr. Sweet employs in his vowel-table may be thus represented in Glossic.

a, as the short vowel corresponding to the first vowel in f*a*ther; compare Glossic [aa], as in [faa·dhur].

æ, as *a* in m*a*n; Glossic [a], as in [man].

è, as *e* in t*e*ll; Glossic [e *or* ae], as in [tel]; provincial [tael].

é, as *ai* in b*ai*t; Glossic [ai], as in [bait].

ə, as *u* in b*u*t; Glossic [u], as in [but].

i, as in b*i*t; Glossic [i], as in [bit].

ò, as in not; òò, as in n*au*ght; Glossic [o] in [not]; [au] in [naut].

ó, as *oa* in b*oa*t; Glossic [oa], as in [boat].

oe, as *ö* in Germ. sch*ö*n; Glossic [oe], as in Germ. [shoen].

u, as *oo* in f*oo*t; uu as *oo* in c*oo*l; Glossic [uo, oo], as in [fuot, kool].

y, as *ü* in Germ. *ü*bel; Glossic [ue], as in Germ. [uebu'l].

ai, a diphthong of a and i, as *y* in m*y*; Glossic [ei], as in [mei].

au, a diphthong of a and u, as *ou* in h*ou*se; Glossic [ou], as in [hous].

éi, a diphthong of é and i, as *a* in *tale*; Glossic [aiy], as in [taiyl].

óu, as *o* in n*o*, i.e. ó with an aftersound of u;[1] Glossic [oaw], as in [noaw].

oi, as *oy* in b*oy*; Glossic [oi], as in [boi].

It may be added, that þ is used to represent the sound of *th* in *thin*, Glossic [thin]; and ð to represent the *th* in *this*, Glossic [dhis].

According, then, to Mr. Sweet's notation, the word *father* is written faaðər; *man*, mæn; *tell*, tèl; *bait*, bét, or (more commonly) béit, in Southern English, béét in Scotch; *but*, bət; *bit*, bit; *not*, nòt; *boat*, bót, or (more commonly) bóut, in Southern English, bóót in Scotch; Germ. *schön*, shoen; *foot*, fut; Germ. *übel*, ybəl; *my*, mai; *house*, haus; *tale*, téil; *no*, nóu; *boy*, boi.

The long vowels are expressed by doubling the symbol employed for the shorter vowels. The following are examples, viz. *father*, faaðer (the short sound of which is found in the Anglo-Saxon *man*, in modern English changed to *mæn*); *earn*, *worse*, əən, wəəs; *saw*, *faught*, sòò, fòòt; *whose*, huuz; and the like. Examples of diphthongs are seen in *eight*, éit; *lord*, *hoarse*, lòəd, hòəs; *smear*, smiər; *bear*, béər; etc.

The easiest way of becoming familiar with this very simple notation is to observe the long list of words beginning at p. 84. By comparing the *third* column, which gives the modern English *spelling*, with the *fourth*, which gives the modern English *pronunciation* according to the above system, the sounds intended can be very easily ascertained, and the reader

[1] More clearly heard when used as a negative, in response to a question, than when used as in the phrase '*no* man.' EXAMPLE: Do you like that? *Answer*—nóu.

will be prepared to understand what is meant by the *first* and *second* columns, which exhibit the pronunciations of the Old and Middle period respectively. The thanks of students are especially due to Mr. Sweet for these word-lists, with the alphabetical register of them appended. They can only have been compiled at the cost of much labour and diligence, and shew an intimate acquaintance with the spellings and pronunciations of all periods of English.

W. W. S.

HISTORY OF ENGLISH SOUNDS.

By HENRY SWEET, Esq.

INTRODUCTION.

In studying the phonetic development of a language two methods are open to us, the historical and the comparative; that is to say, we may either trace the sounds of one and the same language through its successive stages, or else compare the divergent forms in a group of languages which have a common origin.

Each method has its advantages. In the historical method the sequence of the phenomena is self-evident; when we compare two forms of the same sound in several co-existing languages, it is often doubtful which is the older. The peculiar advantage of the comparative method is that it can be applied to living languages, where nothing but careful observation of facts is required, while in the case of dead languages the phonetic material is often defective, and is always preserved in an imperfect form by means of graphic symbols, whose correct interpretation is an indispensable preliminary to further investigation. In short, we may say that the comparative method is based, or may be based, on facts, the historical on theoretical deductions.

It need hardly be said that the first requisite for phonetic investigation of any kind is a knowledge of sounds. Yet nothing is more common in philology than to see men, who have not taken the slightest trouble to make themselves acquainted with the rudiments of vocal physiology, making the boldest and most dogmatic statements about the pronunciation of dead languages—asserting, for instance, that certain sounds are unnatural, or even impossible, merely because they do not happen to occur in their own language. Such prejudices can only be got rid of by a wide and impartial training.

The second requisite is a collection of carefully recorded facts. In this respect the present state of phonology is somewhat anomalous. As far as living languages are concerned, the amount of reliable material that exists is still very small, although it is rapidly increasing, while if we turn to the dead languages we find an enormous body of careful, full, often exhaustive, observations of the varied phenomena of letter-change in the Teutonic languages—a dead mass, which requires the warm breath of living phonology to thaw it into life. Before the word-lists in such a book as Grimm's *Deutsche Grammatik* can be intelligently utilized, the spoken sounds they represent must be determined. The first step is to determine generally the relations between sound and symbol. The ideal of a phonetic notation is, of course, a system in which every simple sound would have a simple sign, bearing some definite relation to the sound it represents. It need hardly be said that all the modifications of the Roman alphabet in which the Teutonic languages have been written down fall far short of this standard. The Roman alphabet was originally, like all naturally developed alphabets, a purely hieroglyphic system, representing not sounds but material objects: the connection of each symbol with its sound is therefore entirely arbitrary. When we consider that this inadequate system was forced on languages of the most diverse phonetic structure, we need not be surprised at the defects of the orthography of the old Teutonic languages, but rather admire the ingenuity with which such scanty resources were eked out.

The maximum of difficulty is reached when a language changes through several generations, while its written representation remains unchanged. In such a case as that of English during the last three centuries, we are compelled to disregard the written language altogether, and have recourse to other methods.

Foremost among these is the study of the contemporary evidence afforded by treatises on pronunciation with their descriptions of the various sounds and comparisons with foreign utterance. It is on this kind of evidence that the well-known investigations of Mr. Ellis are based. The great value of Mr. Ellis's work consists in the impartial and cautious spirit in which he has carried it out, advancing step by step, and never allowing theories to overrule facts. Mr. Ellis's method forms a striking contrast to that pursued by some Early English students, who, starting from the assumption that whatever pronunciation is most agreeable to their own ears must be the right one, take for granted that Alfred, Chaucer, and Shakespere spoke exactly like 19th-century gentlemen, and then, instead of shaping their theories by the existing evidence, pick out those facts which they think confirm their views, and ignore all the rest. The result of Mr. Ellis's investigations is to establish with certainty, within certain limits, the pronunciation of English during the last three centuries; absolute accuracy is impossible in deductions drawn from the vague statements of men who had but an imperfect knowledge of the mechanism of the sounds they uttered.

I hope, however, to show that that minute accuracy which is unattainable by the method adopted by Mr. Ellis, can be reached through a combination of the comparative with the historical method, taking the latter in its widest sense to include both the external evidence employed by Mr. Ellis, and the internal evidence of the graphic forms. This gives us three independent kinds of evidence, which, as we shall see, corroborate each other in the strongest manner.

Before going any farther it will be necessary to say a few words on the phonetic notation I have adopted. The only analysis of vowel-sounds that is of any real use for general scientific purposes is that of Mr. Bell. His system differs from all others in two important particulars, 1) in being based not on the acoustic effects of the sounds, but on their organic formation, and 2) in being of universal applicability: while most other systems give us only a limited number of sounds arbitrarily selected from a few languages, Mr. Bell's *Visible Speech* is entirely independent of any one language—it not only tells us what sounds *do* exist in a given language, but also what sounds *may* exist in any language whatever. It is therefore of priceless value in all theoretical investigations like the present.

The following remarks will help to elucidate Mr. Bell's table of vowels with key-words, which I have given on the opposite page.

Every vowel is, as regards position, either *back* (guttural), of which *aa* is the type, *front* (palatal), typified by *ii*, or *mixed*, that is, formed by the back and front of the tongue simultaneously, as in the English *err*. Each vowel, again, has one of three degrees of elevation—it is either *high*, *mid* or *low*. Each of these nine positions may be *rounded* (labialized). Each of the resulting eighteen vowels must, lastly, be either *narrow*[1] or *wide*. In forming narrow vowels the pharynx or cavity behind the mouth is compressed, while in wide vowels it is relaxed. The distinction will be clearly felt by any one who pronounces *not*, *naught*, several times in succession, drawling them out as much as possible: it will be found that in sounding *not* the pharynx and back of the mouth is relaxed, while in *naught* there is evident tension. The vowel in both words is the low-back-round, but in *not* it is wide, in *naught* narrow.

In treating of the formation of the sounds, I have always described them in Mr. Bell's terminology, which is admirably simple and clear. If I could have made use of his types, I could have avoided a great deal of circumlocution, which, as it is, has proved unavoidable.

For the convenience of those who are not able to appreciate minute phonetic distinctions, I have also adopted a rough practical system of notation, in which only the broadest distinctions are indicated. In this system *a*, *e*, *i*, *o*, *u*, *y*, are employed in their original Roman values, the distinction between open and close *e* and *o* being indicated by accents. To indicate that class of sounds of which the English vowels in *but* and *err* are types, I have adopted the turned *e* (*ə*). The English vowel in *man* is written *æ*, and *æ* is used

[1] I have ventured to substitute "narrow" for Mr. Bell's "primary," as being both shorter and more expressive.

GENERAL VOWEL SCALE.

NARROW.			WIDE.		
1 high-back.	4 high-mixed. *Sw.* upp	7 high-front. *Scotch and occ. Engl.* feel	10 high-back. *occ. Engl.* but *Engl.* eye	13 high-mixed.	16 high-front. *Engl.* bit
2 mid-back. *occ. Eng.* but	5 mid-mixed. *German unacc.* e	8 mid-front. *Dan.* steen *Scotch* take	11 mid-back. *Engl.* father	14 mid-mixed. *Engl.* father	17 mid-front. *occ. Engl.* men *Dan.* læse
3 low-back. *occ. Scotch* but	6 low-mixed. *Eng.* err	9 low-front. *Scotch and occ. Engl.* men	12 low-back. *Sw.* fara *Scotch* man	15 low-mixed *Engl.* how *occ. Scotch* err	18 low-front. *Engl.* man

NARROW-ROUND.			WIDE-ROUND.		
19 high-back. *Scotch and occ. Engl.* fool	22 high-mixed. *Sw.* hus	25 high-front. *Germ.* übel *Dan.* lys	28 high-back. *Eng.* full	31 high-mixed.	34 high-front. *Dan.* synd
20 mid-back. *Germ.* sohn	23 mid-mixed.	26 mid-front. *Dan.* föle *Germ.* schön	29 mid-back. *Engl.* boy *occ. Scotch* no	32 mid-mixed.	35 mid-front. *Dan.* en dör
21 low-back. *Engl.* fall	24 low-mixed.	27 low-front. *Dan.* störst *occ. Germ.* götter	30 low-back. *Engl.* hot	33 low-mixed.	36 low-front.

to designate the German ö. Long vowels are doubled, and diphthongs indicated by combining their elements.[1]

a	as in	f*a*ther	Nos.	11, 12, (3) on Bell's Scale.
æ	,,	m*a*n	,,	18 ,,
è	,,	t*e*ll	,,	9, (17) ,,
é	,,	*Scotch* t*a*le, *French* é	,,	8 ,,
ə	,,	b*u*t, b*i*rd, *German* gab*e*	,,	2, (3), 5, 6, (10), 14, 15.
i	,,	b*i*t, b*ea*t	,,	7, 16.
ò	,,	n*o*t	,,	21, (29), 30 on Bell's Scale.
ó	,,	*Scotch* n*o*te, *Germ.* sohn	,,	20 ,,
œ	,,	*Germ.* schön	,,	(26), 27, 35, 36 ,,
u	,,	w*o*lf	,,	19, 28.
y	,,	*Germ.* *ü*bel	,,	25, (26), 34 ,,
ai	,,	m*y*, *Germ.* m*ei*n.		
au	,,	h*ou*se, *Germ.* h*au*s.		
éi	,,	t*a*le.		
óu	,,	n*o*.		
oi	,,	b*oy*.		

I have not made any use of Mr. Ellis's "palæotype," as, in spite of its typographical convenience, its extreme complexity and arbitrariness make it, as I can testify from personal experience, quite unfitted for popular exposition. The apparent easiness of palæotype as compared with the Visible Speech letters of Mr. Bell is purely delusive: it is certain that those who find Visible Speech too difficult will be quite unable really to master palæotype. It must also be borne in mind that no system of notation will enable the student to dispense with a thorough study of the sounds themselves: there is no royal road to phonetics.

General Laws of Sound Change.

They may be investigated both deductively, that is, by examining known changes in languages, and à priori, by considering the relations of sounds among themselves. I propose to combine these methods as much as possible. Although in giving examples of the various changes I have been careful to select cases which may be considered as perfectly well established, I must in many cases ask the reader to suspend his judgment till they have been fully discussed, which, of course, cannot be done till we come to the details. The general laws I am about to state may, for the present,

[1] Numbers within parentheses indicate the less distinctive vowels, which admit of being brought under different heads: 26, for instance, may be regarded either as a very open *y* or a close *œ*.

be regarded simply as convenient heads for classing the various changes under.

All the changes may be brought under three grand divisions, 1) *organic*, 2) *imitative*, and 3) *inorganic*. Organic changes are those which are the direct result of certain tendencies of the organs of speech: all the changes commonly regarded as weakenings fall under this head. Imitative changes are the result of an unsuccessful attempt at imitation. Inorganic changes, lastly, are caused by purely external causes, and have nothing to do either with organic weakening or with unsuccessful imitation.

The great defect of most attempts to explain sound-changes is that they select some one of these causes, and attempt to explain everything by it, ignoring the two others. It would, for instance, be entirely misleading to explain the change of the O.E. *bær* (pret. of *beran*) into the N.E. *bore* as an organic sound-change, the truth being that the form *bore* is the result of confusion with the participle *borne*. Such a case as this is self-evident, but I hope to show hereafter that the very remarkable and apparently inexplicable changes which our language underwent during the transition from the Old to the Middle period, can be easily explained as inorganic developments.

We may now turn to the two first classes of changes, organic and imitative. From the fact that all sounds are originally acquired by imitation of the mother and nurse we are apt to assume that all sound-change is due to imitation, but a little consideration will show that this is not the case. How, for instance, can such a change as that of a stopped to an open consonant, or of *ii*, *uu*, into *ai*, *au*, be explained by imitation? The fact that the vast majority of those who speak even the most difficult languages *do* make the finest distinctions perfectly well, proves clearly that the correct imitation of sounds is no insurmountable difficulty even to people of very ordinary capacity. The real explanation of such changes as those cited above is that the sounds were acquired properly by imitation, and then modified by the speaker himself, either from carelessness or indolence.

Further confirmation is afforded by the fact, which any one may observe for himself, that most people have double pronunciations, one being that which they learned by imitation, the other an unconscious modification. If asked to pronounce the sound distinctly, they will give the former sound, and will probably disown the other as a vulgarism, although they employ it themselves invariably in rapid conversation. When the habits are fixed, the difficulty of correct imitation largely increases. To the infant one sound is generally not more difficult than another, but to the adult a strange sound is generally an impossibility, or, at any rate, a very serious difficulty. He therefore naturally identifies it with the nearest equivalent in his own language, or else analyses it, and gives the two elements successively instead of simultaneously. We may, therefore, expect a much wider range of the imitative principle in words derived from other languages. I propose, accordingly, to class all the doubtful changes under the head of organic, treating as imitative changes only those which do not allow of any other explanation, but admitting that some of the changes considered as inorganic may under special circumstances be explained as imitative.

Organic sound-changes fall naturally into two main divisions, *simple* and *complex*. Simple changes are those which affect a single sound without any reference to its surroundings, while complex changes imply two sounds in juxtaposition, which modify one another in various ways.

It is generally assumed by philologists that all organic sound-changes may be explained by the principle of economy of exertion, and there can be no doubt that many of the changes must be explained in this way and in no other, as, for instance, the numerous cases of assimilation, where, instead of passing completely from one sound to another, the speaker chooses an intermediate one. Other changes, however, not only do not require this hypothesis of muscular economy, but even run quite counter to it, as when an open consonant is converted into a stop, a by no means uncommon phenomenon in the Teutonic languages. It is of the greatest importance that these exceptions to the general rule should not be suppressed.

I shall, therefore, while giving precedence to those changes which seem to be in harmony with the general principle of economy of force, take care to state fully the exceptions. I begin with the simple changes, arranging them in classes, according to the different vocal organs concerned in their formation.

A. Simple Changes.

I. Weakening.

1) Glottal: voice to whisper and breath. In the formation of voice the glottis is momentarily closed, in that of whisper its edges are only approximated, and in breath the glottis is quite open. It is evident, therefore, that voice *per se* demands the most and breath the least muscular exertion, and that the natural tendency would be to substitute whisper and breath for voice whenever possible. The great preservative of consonantal vocality is the principle of assimilation, to which we shall return presently. When a voice consonant is flanked by vowels, as in *aba*, *aga*, etc., it is much easier to let the voice run on uninterruptedly than to cut it off at the consonant and then resume it. But at the end of a word this assimilative influence is not felt, and accordingly we find that in nearly all the Teutonic languages except English, many of the final voice consonants become either voiceless or whispered.

2) Pharyngal: narrow to wide. In the formation of narrow vowels the pharynx is compressed, while in that of wide vowels it is relaxed. The natural tendency would therefore be from narrow to wide. It is, however, a curious fact that in the Teutonic languages short and long vowels follow diametrically opposed laws of change as regards these pharyngal modifications, long vowels tending to narrowing, short to widening. Full details will be given hereafter; I merely call attention to these Teutonic changes as a clear instance of inapplicability of the principle of economy of force.[1]

3) Changes of position. The most general feature of

[1] Mr. H. Nicol, however, suggests that the narrowing of long vowels may be caused by the effort required to sustain a uniform sound—hence long vowels are either narrowed or diphthongized.

changes of position is the tendency to modify the back articulations, whether vowels or consonants, by shifting forwards to the front, point or lip positions. This is clearly a case of economy of exertion, as the back formations require a movement of the whole body of the tongue, the front and point of only a portion of it. Of the two last the front, on the same principle, evidently require more exertion than the point sounds. The lip consonants (the labial vowels must be reserved), lastly, involve the minimum of exertion.

I will now give a few examples of these various changes.

a) back to front: Sanskrit *ch* (front-stop) from *k*, as in *vach*=*vak;* English *mæn*, *fèèər*, from the Old E. *mann*, *faran*.

b) back to point: E. *méit* from O.E. *gemaca*.

c) back to lip: seems doubtful, as the cases usually cited, such as Greek *pénte*=*kankan*, seem to be the result of the assimilative influence of the *w*-sound preserved in the Latin *quinque*.

d) front to point: the development of *tsh* from *k* through an intermediate front position, as in the E. *church* from *cyrice*; the change of Sanskrit *ç*, as in *çru*, which was originally the voiceless consonant corresponding to the English consonant *y*, to the present sound of *sh*.

e) front and point to lip?[1]

f) back and front to mixed (applies only to vowels). All unaccented vowels in most of the Teutonic languages have been levelled under one sound—the mid-mixed-narrow, as in the German *endə*, *geebən*, from the older *andi*, *giban*.

There are many exceptions to these general tendencies. Thus, of the two *r*s, the back and the point, the former seems to require less exertion than the latter, and hence is often substituted for it in the careless pronunciation of advanced communities, especially in large cities. Other cases, however, really seem to run counter to the principle of economy of force. Such are the change of *th* into

[1] The not unfrequent change of *th* into *f* is no doubt purely imitative (*fruu* for *þruu*).

kh (=German *ch*) in the Scotch (Lothian dialect) *khrii* for *thrii*.

The changes of height in the vowels cannot be brought under any general laws. In the Teutonic languages, at least, short and long vowels follow quite opposite courses, long vowels tending to high, short to low positions.

4) Relaxation:

a) stopped consonants to unstopped: Latin *lingua* from *dingua*; German *makhən* = E. *méik*, *wasər* = *wòòtər*; Modern Greek *dhédhoka* from *dédooka*.

b) unstopped to diphthongal vowel: Middle English *dai*, *lau*, from older *dagh*, *laghu*; English *hiiə* from *hiir*.

c) untrilling: a common phenomenon in most of the Teutonic languages, especially English, in which the trilled *r* is quite lost.

There are some unmistakable exceptions to these tendencies. All the Teutonic languages except English seem to find the *th* and *dh* difficult, and convert them into the corresponding stopped *t* and *d*. In Swedish the *gh* of the oldest documents has, in like manner, become *g*. There seem to be cases of vowels developing into consonants, which will be treated of hereafter. Lastly, we may notice the not unfrequent development of trilled out of untrilled consonants, as in Dutch, where *g* first became opened into *gh*, which in many Dutch dialects has become a regular guttural *r*.

5) Rounding (vowel-labialization). We must distinguish between the rounded back and the rounded front vowels, for their tendencies are directly opposed to one another: back vowels tend to rounding, front to unrounding. In the case of back vowels, rounding may be regarded as an attempt to diminish the expenditure of muscular energy, by keeping the mouth half-closed, whence the change of *aa* into *òò*, which, as we shall see, is almost universal in the Teutonic languages. But with the more easily-formed front vowels this economy of exertion is superfluous: we find, accordingly, that front vowels are seldom rounded, but that rounded front vowels are often unrounded, *y* and *œ* becoming *i* and *e*—a frequent change in the Teutonic languages.

II. Loss.

1) of vowels. The loss of unaccented final vowels is a frequent pheuomenon in all languages. The dropping of final *e* is a characteristic feature of the Modern period of English.

2) of consonants. Here we may distinguish several classes of changes. A single consonant may fall off either before a vowel or a consonant, and it may be initial, medial, or final. The Teutonic languages are, as a general rule, remarkable for the extreme tenacity with which they retain their consonants, especially when final.

B. Complex Changes

III. Influence.

1) One-sided Influence. Influence of one sound on another may be either partial (modification) or complete (assimilation). We must further distinguish the influence of vowel on vowel, vowel on consonant, consonant on consonant, and consonant on vowel.

The modification of one vowel by another, commonly called *umlaut*, is a very important feature of Teutonic sound-change. The following are the most important Teutonic umlauts, which I have formulated as equations.

a...i=è : *O.E.* ènde=*Gothic* andi ; *O. Icelandic* wèèri=waari.
a...u=ò : *O. Icelandic* mònnum=mannum, sòòr=saaru (*pl. of* saar).
i...a=é : *O.E.* stélan=*Gothic* stilan.
u...a=ó : *O.E.* óft=*Gothic* ufta.
u...i=y : *O.E.* fyllan=fullian, myys=muusi.
ó...i=œ : *O E.* grœœne=gróóni.

There are also umlauts of diphthongs, such as *èy* in the Old Icelandic *lèysa*=*lausian.*

The change of *ai* into *èi* in Old Icelandic (*vèit*=*vait*), and the further change of *èi* into *éi* in Modern Icelandic, are examples of what might be called diphthongic umlaut.

It is clear that in all these umlauts the new vowel is exactly intermediate between the original vowel of the root and the modifying one of the termination: if the new vowel became identical with its modifier, the result would be not an umlaut but a complete assimilation. In the Old Icelandic *skǫpuðu=skapaðu* the first vowel is modified, the second assimilated by the final *u*.

Vowel influence on consonants is not very common, but the different forms of German *ch*, after back, front, and rounded vowels, as in *ach*, *ich*, *auch*, are instances of it.

Consonant influence on consonants is very strongly developed in some languages: what is called *sandhi* in Sanskrit and *mutation* in the Celtic languages falls partly under this head. The Teutonic languages, on the other hand, are remarkable for the independence of their consonants, and the freedom with which they are combined without modifying one another. Consonant influence on vowels, lastly, is perhaps the obscurest of all phonetic problems: the explanation of its varied phenomena seems to require a far greater knowledge of the synthesis of speech-sounds than is at present attained by phonologists. These influences are strongly developed both in Old and Modern English, and will be treated of in their place.

The converse of the processes just considered is *dissimilation*, by which two identical sounds are made unlike, or two similar sounds are made to diverge. The development of the Teutonic preterite *wista* out of *witta* is an example of consonantal, the diphthongization of *ii* into *éi* in Early Modern English of vowel dissimilation, while the further change of *éi* into *əi* and *ai* is a case of divergence of similar sounds. The whole phenomena of *dissimilation* is anomalous, and it is doubtful whether many of the instances ought not to be ascribed to purely external causes, as, for instance, the desire of greater clearness.

2) Mutual Influence. Mutual influence, in which *both* the sounds are modified by one another, may be either partial or complete. I do not know of any sure instance of partial convergence.

The commonest type of complete convergence is such a change as that of *au* into *òò*, in which two distinct sounds are simplified into one sound different from and yet similar to both of them. This simplification of diphthongs is, as we shall see, a very frequent phenomenon in the history of English sounds. Of consonantal simplification we have an example in the English *wh* in *what*, which was first *khwat*, then *h-wat*, and lastly *what*, the initial *h* being incorporated into the *w*, which consequently lost its vocality.

The converse phenomenon of divergence is exemplified in the resolution of simple long vowels into diphthongs. We have seen that *òò* is often the result of the simplification of *au*, but in Icelandic the process has been reversed—the Old Icelandic *òò* (as in *dòòð* from *daað*) has become *au*. In the same way the Middle English *yy* has in the present English been resolved into *iu*. Whether short vowels are ever resolved is very doubtful.

IV. Transposition.

Transposition may be of consonants, as in the familiar *æx* for *ask*, or else of vowels in different syllables, as in the Greek *meinō* for *meniō*. This latter case must be carefully distinguished from umlaut. There seem also to be cases of transposition in different words, or in whole classes of words, such as the confusion between *'air=hair* and *hair=air*, which seems to be often made in the London dialect.

The results obtained may be conveniently summed up thus:

A. Simple Changes.

I. Weakening.

1) Glottal: voice to whisper and breath.
2) Pharyngal: narrow to wide.
3) Position: a) back to front.
   b) back to point.
   c) back to lip?
   d) front to point.

e) front and point to lip?
f) back and front to mixed (vowels only).
g) vowel-height?

4) Relaxation: a) stop to unstopped; b) unstopped to vowel; c) untrilling.

5) Vowel-rounding: rounding of back; unrounding of front.

II. Loss.

1) Of vowels: unaccented final *e*.

2) Consonants: before vowel, before another consonant; initial, medial, final.

B. Complex Changes

III. Influence.

1) One-sided, a) convergent:
partial (modification), complete (assimilation); vowel on vowel (umlaut), vowel on consonant, consonant on consonant (sandhi), consonant on vowel.
b) divergent (dissimilation): of vowels, of consonants.

2) Mutual, a) convergent:
partial (diphthongic umlaut), complete (diphthongic simplification); consonantal.
b) divergent: resolution of long vowels, of short (?).

IV. Transposition.

1) Of consonants.
2) Of vowels (in different syllables).
3) In different words.

Imitative Sound-Changes.

The general principle on which imitative changes depend is simply this—that the same effect, or nearly the same, may be produced on the ear by very different means. Thus, starting from the mid-front-narrow vowel *e*, we can lower its natural pitch either by slightly raising the back of the tongue, and thus producing the corresponding mixed *ə* instead of the front vowel, or else by rounding into the mid-front-round *œ*, the result being that *œ* and *ə* are so alike in sound that they are constantly confused in many languages. This similarity of sound between the mixed and round vowels was first pointed out by Mr. Bell (Visible Speech, p. 87).

There is the same similarity between the low-narrow and the mid-wide vowels, and also between the high-wide and the mid-narrow. Thus the English *e* in *men* is indifferently pronounced, either as the mid-front-wide or the low-front-narrow, and the *ə* in *bət* as the high-back-wide or the mid-back-narrow.

Whenever, then, we find a sound changing directly into another which, although very similar in acoustic effect, is formed in quite a different manner, we may be sure that the change is an imitative, not an organic one. Thus, when we find *œ* and *ə* constantly interchanging without any intermediate stages, it would be unreasonable to assume, as we should have to do on the assumption of organic change, three such stages as *œ*, *é*, *ə*, whereas the imitative hypothesis makes the direct change of *œ* into *ə* perfectly intelligible.

Inorganic Changes.

Inorganic sound-changes, which result from purely external causes, are of a very varied character, and are consequently difficult to classify. One of the most prominent of these external influences is the striving after logical clearness, which comes more and more into play as the sounds of the language become less distinct. Clearness may again be attained in many ways—by discarding one of two words which have run together in form, though distinct in meaning, or by taking advantage of any tendency to change which may keep the two words distinct (scheideformen). The phenomenon of *levelling*, by which advanced languages get rid of superfluous distinctions, is a very important inorganic change, and is strongly developed in Transition English. A familiar aspect of inorganic sound-change is the alteration of foreign words so as to give them a homely appearance, as in *sparrow-grass* for *asparagus*.

General Law of Change.

The investigation of the various laws of sound-change—important as it is—must not be allowed to divert our attention from the general principle on which they all depend, namely that of incessant change—alternations of development and decay. To say that language changes looks very like a truism, but if so, it is a truism whose consequences are very generally ignored by theorizers on pronunciation. The most important lesson that it teaches us is to regard all cases of stand-still, whether of phonetic or of general linguistic development, as abnormal and exceptional. These cases of arrested development are really much rarer than is commonly supposed, and many of them are quite delusive—the result of the retention of the written representation of an older language, from which the real living language has diverged widely. English and Icelandic are striking examples. The written English language is for all practical purpose an accurate representation of the spoken language of the sixteenth century, which, as far as the sounds themselves are concerned, is as different from the present English as Latin is from Italian. The apparent stability of our language during the last few centuries is purely delusive.

The case of English and Icelandic also shows how it is possible for a language to retain its grammatical structure unimpaired, and at the same time to undergo the most sweeping changes in its phonetic system. How much more then are we bound to expect a change of pronunciation where the whole grammatical structure of a language has been subverted!

It is not only in its unceasing alternations of development and decay that language shows its analogy with the other manifestations of organic life, but also in another very important feature, namely in that of increasing complexity of phonetic structure. The greater number of sounds in a late as opposed to an early language is at once evident on comparing two languages belonging to the same stock, but in different stages of development, such as English with German, French with Italian or Spanish. It can further be shown that even in German, in its sounds one of the most archaic of the living Teutonic languages, many of the simple vowels are of comparatively late origin.

The sounds of early languages, besides being few in number, are more sharply marked off, more distinct than those of their descendants. Compare the multitude of indistinct vowel sounds in such a language as English with the clear simplicity of the Gothic and Sanskrit triad *a*, *i*, *u*—the three most distinct sounds that could possibly be produced. From these three vowels the complex systems of the modern languages have been developed by the various changes already treated of.

There can be little doubt that the simplicity of earlier phonetic systems was partly due to want of acoustic discrimination, and that primitive Man contented himself with three vowels, simply because he would have been unable to distinguish between a larger number of sounds. The really marvellous fineness of ear displayed by those who speak such languages as English, Danish, or French, must be the result of the accumulated experience of innumerable generations.

From this we can easily deduce another law, namely that the changes in early languages are not gradual, but *per saltum*. A clear appreciation of this principle is of considerable importance, as many philologists have assumed that in such changes as that of a back into a front consonant (Sanskrit *k* into *ch*) the tongue was shifted forwards by imperceptible gradations. Such assumptions are quite unnecessary, besides being devoid of proof. To people accustomed previously only to the broad distinction between back and point consonant, the further distinction of front must at first have appeared almost indistinguishable from its two extremes.

Under such circumstances it is not easy to see how they could have distinguished intermediate modifications of the original sound.

General Alphabetics.

Although it would be possible to carry on the present investigation on a purely comparative basis—confining our attention exclusively to the living languages—such a process would prove tedious and difficult, if pursued without any help from the historical method, many of whose deductions are perfectly well established: to ignore these would be perverse pedantry. But the historical method must be based on a study of the graphic forms in which the older languages are preserved, and especially of their relation to the sounds they represent. It is quite useless to attempt to draw deductions from the spelling of a language till we know on what principles that spelling was formed. We have only to look at living languages to see how greatly the value of the spelling of each language varies. In English and French the spelling is almost worthless as a guide to the actual language; in German and Spanish the correspondence between sound and symbol is infinitely closer, and in some languages, such as Finnish and Hungarian, it is almost perfect—as far as the radical defects of the Roman alphabet allow.

With these facts before us, it is clearly unreasonable to assume, as many philologists have done, that the same divergence between orthography and pronunciation which characterizes Modern English prevailed also in the earlier periods, and consequently that no reliable deductions can be drawn from the graphic forms. I feel confident that every one who has patience enough to follow me to the end of the present discussion will be convinced of the very opposite. Putting aside the actual evidence altogether, it is quite clear that the wretched attempts at writing the sounds of our dialects made by educated men of the present day cannot be taken as standards from which to infer a similar result a thousand years ago.

An educated man in the nineteenth century is one who

has been taught to associate groups of type-marks with certain ideas: his conception of language is visual, not oral. The same system is applied to other languages as well as English, so that we have the curious phenomenon of people studying French and German for twenty years, and yet being unable to understand a single sentence of the spoken languages; also of Latin verses made and measured by eye, like a piece of carpentry, by men who would be unable to comprehend the metre of a single line of their own compositions, if read out in the manner of the ancients. The study of Egyptian hieroglyphics affords almost as good a phonetic training as this.

Before the invention of printing the case was very different. The Roman alphabet was a purely phonetic instrument, the value of each symbol being learned by ear, and consequently the sounds of the scribe being also written by ear. The scarcity of books, the want of communication between literary men, and the number of literary dialects—all these causes made the adoption of a rigid, unchanging orthography a simple impossibility. It must not, of course, be imagined that there were *no* orthographical traditions, but it may be safely said that their influence was next to none at all. The only result of greater literary cultivation in early times was to introduce a certain roughness and carelessness in distinguishing shades of sound: we shall see hereafter that sounds which were kept distinct in the thirteenth-century spelling were confused in the time of Chaucer, although it is quite certain that they were still distinguished in speech. But such defects, although inconvenient to the investigator, do not lead him utterly astray, like the retention of a letter long after the corresponding sound has changed or been lost, which is so often the case in orthographies fixed on a traditional basis.

Early scribes not only had the advantage of a rational phonetic tradition—not a tradition of a fixed spelling for each word, but of a small number of letters associated each with one sound;—but, what is equally important, the mere practical application of this alphabet *forced* them to observe and analyse the sounds they wrote down: in short they were trained to habits of phonetic observation. Yet another advantage was possessed by the earliest scribes—that of a comparatively limited number of sounds to deal with. For the proofs of this position I must refer to the remarks I have made in the discussion of the Laws of Sound Change, and to the details of the investigation itself.

The Roman alphabet consisted of six simple vowel signs, a e i o u y: on these six letters the vowel notation of all the Teutonic languages was based. If, therefore, we can determine the sounds attached to these letters by the Romans during the first few centuries of Christianity, we can also determine, within certain limits, the sounds of the unlettered tribes who adopted the Roman alphabet to write their own languages. Nor need our determination be absolutely accurate. It is certain that minute shades of difference between a Latin and, for example, an Old English sound would not have deterred the first writers of English from adopting the letter answering to the Latin sound: all that was wanted was a distinctive symbol.

Now there can be no doubt as to the general values of the six Roman vowel-signs. The sounds of the first five are still preserved in nearly all the Modern Latin languages, and that of the *y*, although lost in Italian and the other cognate languages, can be determined with certainty from the descriptions of the Latin grammarians, and from its being the regular transcription of the Greek *upsilon*. The values of the Roman vowel-letters may, then, be represented approximately thus:

a=Italian	*a*;	English	f*a*ther.
e	,,	*e*	,,	bed, be*a*r.
i	,,	*i*	,,	b*i*t, be*a*t.
o	,,	*o*	,,	odd, bore.
u	,,	*u*	,,	f*u*ll, f*oo*l.
y=French	*u*;	Danish	*y*.

We see that even in English the traditional values of the Roman letters have been very accurately preserved in many cases, and it need hardly be said that the majority of the living Teutonic languages have preserved them almost as faithfully as Italian and Spanish. We thus find that the Romance and Teutonic traditions are in complete harmony after a lapse of more than ten centuries. The greatest number of exceptions to the general agreement occur in the two most advanced languages of each group—English and French; but it can be shown that these divergences are of very late origin, and that in the sixteenth century the original tradition was still maintained.

We may now pass from the consideration of the single letters to that of their combinations or digraphs. The first use of digraphs, namely to express diphthongs, is self-evident, but they have a distinct and equally important function in symbolizing simple sounds which have no proper sign in the original Roman alphabet. The plan adopted was to take the symbols of two different sounds which both resembled the one in question, and write them one after the other, implying, however, that they were to be pronounced not successively but simultaneously—that an intermediate sound was to be formed. Thus, supposing there had been no *y* in the Roman alphabet, the sound might still have been easily represented by writing *u* and *i* (or *e*) together, implying an intermediate sound, which is no other than that of *y*. As we see, the framers of the Old English alphabet, living at a time when the Roman *y* still had its original sound, had no need of this expedient; but in Germany, where the sound of *y* did not develope till a comparatively late period—during the twelfth century—the only course open was to resort to a digraph, so that the sound which in Danish is still expressed by the Old Roman *y*, is in Modern German written *ue*.

This *ue* affords at the same time an excellent example of the way in which diacritical modifications are developed out of digraphs. The first step is to write one of the two letters above or under the other: accordingly we find the German *ue* in later times written *ů*. Afterwards the *e* was further abbreviated into two dots, giving the familiar *ü*. In some cases the diacritic becomes incorporated into the letter, and there results what is practically an entirely new letter. Although most diacritics can be explained in this way, as corruptions of originally independent letters, there are still a few cases of arbitrary modification, of which the Old English ð from *d* is an example. Cases of the arbitrary use of consonants as digraphic modifiers also occur. Thus *h* has come to be a perfectly unmeaning sign, implying any imaginable modification of the consonant it is associated with. Compare *g* and *gh* in Italian, *l* and *lh* in Portuguese, etc. The doubling of consonants to express new sounds is equally arbitrary, as in the Welsh *ff* as distinguished from *f*, and the Middle English *ss*=*sh*.

In all the cases hitherto considered the digraph is formed consciously and with design, but it often happens that a diphthong becomes simplified, and the original digraph is still retained for the sake of distinctness. Thus, if the diphthong *iu* passes into the simple sound of *yy*, it is clearly the simplest and most practical course to retain the *iu*, as being a perfectly legitimate representation of a sound which, although simple, lies between *i* and *u*.

All diacritical letters, whatever their origin, are distinguished in one very important respect from the older digraphs —they are perfectly unambiguous, while it is often difficult to determine whether a given digraph is meant to represent a diphthong or a simple sound. There is, however, one invariable criterion, although, unfortunately, it cannot always be applied, which is *the reversibility of the elements of the digraph*. Thus, the sound written *oe* in Old English, as in *boec* (later *bec*), might, on the evidence of this spelling alone, be taken equally well for a diphthongic combination of *o* and *e*, or for a sound intermediate to these two vowels; but when we find *boec* and *beoc* alternating, as they do, on the same page, we see that the *e* was a mere modifier, whose position before or after the vowel to be modified was quite immaterial: the sound must therefore have been simple—a conclusion which is fully confirmed by other evidence.

The Roman alphabet has been further enriched by the differentiation of various forms of the same letter, of which the present distinctions between *u* and *v*, *i* and *j*, are instances. In these cases varieties of form which were originally purely ornamental and arbitrary have been ingeniously utilized to express distinctions in sounds.

Quantity and Quality in the Teutonic Languages.

The distinguishing feature of the early Teutonic languages is the important part played in them by quantity. This subject has been very fully investigated by Grimm and his school in Germany, and it may be regarded as proved beyond a doubt that in the Teutonic languages quantity was originally quite independent of stress or quality, and that many words were distinguished solely by their quantity.

Even so late as the thirteenth century we find the German poetry regulated partly by quantitative laws. Not only are short and long vowels never rhymed together, but there is also a fine distinction made between dissyllables with short and long penultimates; words like *bite* (modern *bitte*) being treated as metrically equivalent to a monosyllable, while *rîte* (now *reite*) is regarded as a true dissyllable. Many metres which employ monosyllabic rhyme-words indifferently with words like *bite* do not show a single instance of a dissyllable like *rîte* at the end of the line.

Similar instances may be adduced from the Icelandic rímur of the fourteenth and fifteenth centuries.

All this is fully confirmed by the direct evidence of many German MSS. of the eleventh century, which employ the circumflex regularly to denote a long vowel.

It is further generally admitted that in the living Teutonic languages these distinctions have mostly vanished, short vowels before single consonants having been generally lengthened, and that quantitative distinctions have been replaced by qualitative ones. The general laws, however, on which these changes depend, have not hitherto been investigated, and I propose hereafter to treat of them in some detail: at present we must content ourselves with an examination of the more general features of the change.

In the substitution of qualitative for quantitative distinctions we can easily observe three stages, 1) the purely quantitative, 2) the transitional, in which, while the distinctions of quantity are still preserved, short and long vowels begin to diverge qualitatively also, and 3) the qualitative, in which long and short vowels are confounded, so that the original quantitative distinctions are represented, if at all, by quality only.

That the oldest English still retained the original quantitative system is in itself highly probable from the analogy of the other cognate languages, and also admits of decisive proof. If we take two vowels, one originally long, the other originally short, which are both long and yet qualitatively distinct in the living language, and show that they were qualitatively identical at an earlier period, we are forced to assume a purely quantitative distinction, for the later divergence of quality could not have developed out of nothing. Let us take the words *stoun* and *bein*, written in Old English *stan* and *bana*. It is quite certain that the *a* of *stan* was originally long, for it is nothing but a simplification of an older *ai*, still preserved in the German *shtain*, while there is equally decisive proof of the shortness of the *a* of *bana*. Now, if there had been any difference in the quality of the two vowels, they would certainly not have been written with the same letter. The back vowel *a* can only be modified in two directions—in that of *e* or of *o*, that is, by fronting or rounding, and, as we shall see hereafter, such changes were regularly indicated by a change of spelling, even when the departure from the original sound was very minute. We are, therefore, led to the conclusion that the present purely qualitative distinction between *stoun* and *bein* was in the Old English period purely quantitative—*staan* and *bana*. Similar evidence is afforded by the other vowels.

As we have little direct evidence of the quantity of individual Old English words, recourse must be had to the comparison of the old cognates, for the details of which I must refer to the works of Grimm and his successors in Germany. Much may also be learned from the qualitative distinctions of the modern languages.

OLD ENGLISH PERIOD.

We may now proceed to a detailed examination of the vowel-sounds of our language in its oldest stage. The results of this investigation—which is an indispensable preliminary to the study of the later changes—cannot be properly appreciated till the evidence is fully set forth ; at present I only wish to remind the reader that a rigorously mathematical method is quite impracticable in such an investigation, which can only be carried out by a process of cumulative reasoning, based on a number of independent probabilities. Nothing can be more irrational than to ignore an obvious deduction merely because it is a deduction, or to discard one that, although not absolutely certain, is extremely probable, in favour of another that is only barely possible.

The principle I have adopted in cases of uncertainty is to adopt the oldest sound that can be ascertained. It happens in many cases that although we can say with certainty that a sound underwent a certain change, we cannot point out the exact period in which the new sound arose. It must be borne in mind that the written language, even in the most illiterate and therefore untraditional times, is always somewhat behind the living speech, and further that a new pronunciation may exist side by side with the old for a long time. In such cases it is necessary to have some definite criterion of selection, and that of always taking the oldest sound seems the most reasonable.

Short Vowels.

A (Æ, O).

The short *a* of the cognate languages is in Old English preserved only in certain cases: 1) before a single consonant followed by *a*, *o*, or *u*, which have, however, in the earliest extant period of the language been in some cases weakened into *e* : *hara*, *hagol*, *caru*, *care* ; 2) before nasals: *bana*, *lamb*, *lang*. In other cases *a* is replaced by *æ*: *dæg*, *æppel*, *cræftig*. Alternations of *a* and *æ* according to these rules often occur in various inflexions of the same word: *dæg*, *dæges*, *dagas*, *dagum*. *a* before nasals is liable to interchange with *o*: *bona*, *lomb*, *long*. This *o* is so frequent in the earlier period as in many words almost to supersede the *a*, but afterwards the *a* gets the upper hand, the *o* being preserved in only a few very frequent words, such as *þonne*, *on*, *of*, which last is an exceptional case of *o* developing before *f*, also occurring in the proper name *Offa* (=original *Aba*).

So far goes the evidence of the graphic forms, as it may be found in any comparative grammar, and before bringing in the living languages it will be as well to consider what deductions may be drawn from them. In the first place it is clear that the development of the *æ* is not due to any assimilation, but is a purely negative phenomenon, that is to say, that wherever *a* was not supported by a back vowel in the next syllable, it was weakened into *æ* without any regard to the following consonant. The change cannot therefore, as German philologists have already remarked, be compared to the regular vowel-mutation or umlaut.

As to the pronunciation of this *æ*, the spelling clearly points to a sound intermediate between *a* and *e*, while the joining together of the two letters and the frequent degradation of the *a* into a mere diacritic, which is sometimes entirely omitted, show that it was a simple sound, not a diphthong: further than this we cannot advance till we have determined more accurately the sounds of *a* and *e*.

It is also clear that the *o* of *long*=*lang* must have been distinct from the regular *o* in *gold*, etc., for otherwise they would have run together and been confused. This conclusion is further confirmed by direct graphic evidence. In the riddles of that well-known collection of Old English poetry, the Exeter Book, the solution is sometimes given in Runic letters written backwards, and in one of them occurs the word COFOAH which, read backwards, gives *haofoc*=*hafoc* (hawk). Here we have an *a* labialized before *f*, as in *of*=*af*, written *ao*, with the evident intention of indicating a sound intermediate between *a* and *o*, just as *æ* points to a sound intermediate between *a* and *e*.

We may now turn our attention to the pronunciations of the modern languages. Disregarding minute shades of sound, we may distinguish three kinds of *a*s in the living Teutonic languages:

1) the mid-back-wide: English *father*, ordinary German *a*.

2) the low-back-wide: Scotch short *a* in *man*.

3) the low-back-narrow: I hear this sound in the South German dialects for both long and short *a*, and in Dutch for the short *a*, especially before *l*.

As to the relative antiquity of these sounds, there can be little doubt that the first is a later modification of the second, and it is very probable that the second is a weakened form of the third. In fact, it may safely be said that this last requires more exertion in its utterance than any other vowel —a fact which easily accounts for its rarity, and also for its preservation in the South German dialects, which, as we shall see hereafter, have preserved their short vowels more purely than any of the other languages.

Are we then to assume that the Old English *a* had this narrow sound? Analogy is certainly in favour of this assumption, but a little consideration will show that it is untenable. If *a* had been narrow, its weakening *æ*, which is simply *a* moved on towards *e*, would also have been narrow, giving no other sound than the low-front-narrow; but this, as we shall see, was the sound of the open short *e*, from which the *æ* is kept quite distinct: the *æ*, therefore, cannot have been narrow, nor, consequently, its parent *a*. But if we suppose the *a* to have had the sound of the Scotch *man*— that is the low-wide—the difficulty is cleared away, and we come to the very probable conclusion that the *æ* had the exact sound of the modern English *man*—the low-front-wide.

The *a* if labialized (or rounded) would naturally give the low-back-round-wide (English *not*), and as there is every reason to believe that the normal *o* was the mid-back-round-narrow, we see that the labialized *a* in *monn*, etc., was exactly half-way between *a* and *o*—a conclusion to which we have already been led by an examination of the graphic evidence.

I.

The only debatable point about the *i* is whether it had the wide sound of the English and Icelandic or the narrow of the German and Swedish short *i*. All we can say is that, although it is possible that the wide sound may have been the real one, every analogy is in favour of the narrow.

E.

We must distinguish two kinds of *e*s in the Teutonic languages, 1) the *a*-mutation of *i*, as in *helpan*=Gothic *hilpan*, and 2) the *i*-mutation of *a*, as in *ende*=Gothic and Old High German *andi*. The two sounds are now confounded in the Teutonic languages, but there is clear evidence that they were formerly distinct, for in the Middle High German poetry the two *e*s are never rhymed together, and the Icelander Þóroddr, in his treatise on orthography, carefully distinguishes the two, stating that the *e* from *a* had a sound which was a mixture of *a* and *e*, implying, of course, that the other *e* was nearer to the *i* from which it arose.

It has been generally assumed by comparative philologists that there was no distinction between the two *e*s in Old English, but, as I have pointed out elsewhere,[1] there is unmistakable graphic evidence to prove that there was a distinction, the *e* from *a* being often written *æ*, although this spelling was soon abandoned because of the confusion it caused with the regular *æ* of *dæg*, etc.

Putting all these facts together, rememberıng that the one *e* was nearer *i*, the other nearer *a*, and yet distinct from the *æ*, we can hardly help assigning to the *e* from *i* the sound of the mid-front-narrow, and to the *e* from *a* that of the low-front-narrow. That the *e* from *a* was narrow need not make any difficulty, when we consider that the change took place at a much earlier period than that of the development of the *æ* of *dæg*, etc.—in short, at a period in which the *a* was probably narrow in all the Teutonic languages.

[1] King Alfred's West-Saxon Version of Gregory's Pastoral Care. Introd. p. xxiii.

The unaccented *e* in such words as *gebiden*, *ende*, requires to be considered separately. In all the living Teutonic languages which possess this sound—that is to say, all except Icelandic and English—it is the mid-mixed-narrow. But in many of the South German dialects the mid-front-narrow occurs, which is clearly a more ancient sound. That this was the sound of the Old Icelandic unaccented *e* (now written and pronounced *i*) is clear from Þóroddr's expressly adducing the second vowel of *framer* (=*framir*: nom. plur. masc. of *framr*) as an example of the close *e* arising from *i*.

It seems most reasonable to suppose that this pronunciation, which is also preserved to the present day in South Germany, was also the Old English one.

U.

What has been said of *i* applies equally to *u*, namely that analogy is in favour of its having had the narrow German sound rather than the wide English one.

O.

It is quite clear that the sound now given to the regular short *o* in all the Teutonic languages except German—the low-back-wide-round—cannot be the old one; for, as we have seen, this was the sound of the modified *a* before nasals (*monn*, etc.) which is kept quite distinct from the regular *o* in such a word as *oft*. This latter *o* is nothing else than an *a*-mutation of *u* (compare *oft* with Gothic *ufta*): it seems, therefore, reasonable to suppose that, as the *a*-mutation of *i* differed from the latter vowel simply in being lowered one degree towards the "low" position of the *a*, the *o* was simply the *u* lowered from its high to the mid position, resulting in the mid-back-narrow-round. Now this is the sound still preserved all over South Germany, and until further evidence is forthcoming it seems to me that we are justified in assuming that the same was the Old English sound.

Y.

This letter, which was originally nothing else but a Greek *Υ*, was adopted into the Roman alphabet to denote the sound of the Greek *u*, which did not exist in Latin. The pronunciation of this Greek *u* is generally agreed to have been that of the French *u* or the German *ü*, and it is clear, from the descriptions of the Roman grammarians, that they attached the same value to their *y*, with which the Greek *u* is invariably transcribed. It is a remarkable fact that while the original sound of the Roman *y* has been quite lost in the Romance languages, it is still preserved in Danish and Swedish. As we know that the Scandinavian nations learned the use of the Roman alphabet from England, this Scandinavian tradition not only confirms the generally-received pronunciation of the Roman *y*, but also affords independent proof of the sound of the letter in Old English.

In its origin *y* is the *i*-mutation of *u*; its sound is therefore, as the Icelander Þóroddr says, "blended together of *i* and *u*," and Þóroddr actually considers *y* to be a combination of these two letters. The sound which fulfils these conditions is clearly that which is still preserved in South Germany, Sweden, and, in many words, in Danish—the high-front-narrow-round. This, then, we may safely assume to have been the Old English sound also.

Long Vowels.

AA.

Long *a* in Old English corresponds to an *ai* of the older cognates, Gothic and Old High German, of which it is a simplified form. As the *aa* has been rounded at a later period, and is represented in the present language by the diphthong *ou*, some theorists, who seem incapable of realizing the possibility of sounds changing during the lapse of ten centuries, have assumed that it was labial in the Old English period as well. The answer to this is, that if the sound had been at all labial, it would have been written, at least occasionally, *o* or *oa*, as was actually done at a later period, and as the Old English scribes themselves did in the case of short *a* before nasals: when we find the tenth century scribes writing invariably *stan*, and those of the twelfth century writing as invariably *stoon* or *ston*, it seems simplest to infer that the former meant to indicate *a* and the latter some variety of *o*.

ÆÆ.

There are two long *æ*s in Old English. The commonest is that which corresponds to original *ai*, as in *sǣ*, *dǣl*=Gothic *saiw*, *dail*. The relation of this *ǣ* to the *ā* treated of above is not quite clear. In some words, such as *clǣne*=Old German *kleini*, the *æ* may be explained as an umlaut of *ā*, original *claini* first becoming *clāni* and then *clǣni*. But such words as *sǣ* and *dǣl* do not admit this explanation. It seems therefore simplest to assume that *ǣ* and *ā* are both independent modifications of *ai*, the former being formed by convergence, the latter by loss of the *i*.

The second *ǣ* is that which corresponds to original *ā*, Gothic *ē*, as in *dǣd*=Gothic *dēd*, Old German *tāt*. It is, however, quite clear (as will be shown hereafter) from the Modern English forms that this *ǣ* did not exist in the dialect from which literary English has arisen, but was represented by *ē*, as in Gothic, which is the case even in the West-Saxon in some words, such as *wēn*=Old German *wān*, Gothic *wēn*, and the proper name *Ælfrēd*=Old German *Alprāt*.

The only question about the sound of *ǣ* is whether it was narrow or wide. The analogy of short *æ* would rather point to its being wide, that of the pronunciation of Modern German, in which the *èè*-umlaut of *ā* (*kèèzə*=*kaasi*) is always narrow, rather to narrowness. In fact the long sound of the *æ* in *mæn* is quite unknown in the Modern Teutonic languages. It must also be borne in mind that *ǣ* is probably a much older formation than the short *æ*, and may very well have been developed at a time when all the vowels were still narrow. If so, long *æ* must have been the low-front-narrow.

EE.

Long *ē* corresponds first to original *ā*, although, as already stated, this *ē* often becomes *ǣ* in the West-Saxon dialect. In many words it is a simplification of the diphthongs *eā* and *eō*, as in *nēd, ēc*=*neād, eāc* (both of which forms are also common), *gēng*=*geōng*. The third and most common *ē* is the *i*-umlaut of *ō*, written *oe* in the oldest documents, as in *grēne* (*groene*)= original *grōni*. The pronunciation of all these *ē*s was probably the same, as they are not distinguished from one another in writing, and cannot well have been any other than the mid-front-narrow.

II, UU,

Correspond to original *ii* and *uu*, which are still preserved in the Scandinavian languages, the Old English *wīn* and *hūs* being now pronounced in Icelandic and Danish *viin, huus*. There can be no doubt that the Old English sounds were the same as those still preserved in these languages—the high-front-narrow and the high-back-narrow-round.

OO

Corresponds to original *ō*, as in *gōd, mōdor*. The sound was no doubt the same as that still preserved in Danish and Swedish, namely the mid-back-narrow-round, but without the abnormal rounding of the *óó* of these languages.[1]

YY

Is the umlaut of *ū*, as in *mȳs* = *mūsi*, plural of *mūs*. In some words, such as *fȳr* (Old German *viuwar*), it is a simplification of *iu* by diphthongal convergence. Its pronunciation cannot well have been anything else than the high-front-narrow-round.

Diphthongs.

EA.

Whenever original *a* comes before consonant-combinations beginning with *l*, *r*, or *h*, it is not changed into *æ*, but becomes *ea*, as in *eall, wearm, weax*. There can be no doubt that this *ea* was a true diphthong: its elements are never reversed (p. 23), nor is it confounded with *ae* or *æ*. The only question is whether the stress was

[1] See my paper on Danish Pronunciation (Trans. Phil. Soc. 1873-4, p. 101).

on the first or the second element. There is evidence which seems to point to the conclusion that the stress fell on the *a*. In Middle English *ea* is generally lost, but in the archaic fourteenth century Kentish of the Ayenbite, the old diphthong is still preserved in such words as *eald*, *healden*. But this *ea* is very often represented by *ya*, sometimes by *yea*, so that the Old English *eald* appears as *eald*, *yald* and *yeald*. Here we have the glide-vowel represented by the Middle English consonant *y*, showing clearly that the stress was on the *a*. As to the origin of the *ea*, the theory first propounded by Rapp (Physiologie der Sprache, ii. 145) seems the most probable, namely that *a* first became *æ* before *all* consonants (except nasals), so that *ald* became *æld*, and that this *æ* was then diphthongized into *ea* or rather *æa*.

EO.

Similarly, when *é* comes before *r*, *l* and *h*-combinations, it is diphthongized into *eo*, as in *eorðe*, *meolc*, *feoh*. In the Kentish and Northumbrian documents this *eo* is generally represented by *ea*, *eorðe* being written *earðe*. In the word *eart* (from *ért*) *eo* never occurs in any of the dialects—the normal *eort* being unknown even in West-Saxon. When we consider that *é* in Icelandic also is changed into *ia* (*ea* in the oldest MSS.), as in *hiarta*=Old E. *heorte*, there seems to be every probability that *ea* was the older sound, which in *eart* was preserved in all the dialects, on account of its excessive frequency. As *eo* is never (except in *eart*) confused with *ea*=*a* in the standard West-Saxon, we must suppose that the series of changes, *é*, *ea*, *eo*, was already completed when *ea*=*a* began to develope itself. The rounding of *ea* into *eo* is a very curious phenomenon. The frequent rounding of vowels before *l*, of which the Modern English *sòlt* from *salt* is an instance, would lead us to suppose that the change first began before *l*, and then extended to the other words. The analogy of Modern Icelandic, in which the first element of the *ia* has developed into a consonant, and of the Middle Kentish *y* in *yald*, make it very probable that the stress was on the second element.

EAA.

Besides the *ea* from *a*, there is another *ea*, which answers to original *au*, as in *dream*=Gothic *draum*. As this *ea* is distinct in origin and in subsequent development from the other *ea*, it must have been distinct in sound. The only conceivable distinctions are stress and quantity, that is, the *ea*=*au* may have been distinguished either by having the stress on the first element, or else by its accented vowel being long. The former supposition is made untenable by both the Middle Kentish *ya*, as in *dyaþ*, and the Norse spelling *Iatvarðr*(=*Játvarðr*) for *Eadweard*: these examples show that *ea*=*au* had the stress on the same vowel as *ea*=*a*. We are driven, therefore, to the hypothesis that *ea*=*au* had its second element long—*dreaam*. This view is confirmed by the Modern English form of the preterite *ceās* (Gothic *kaus*) which is *chóóz*—an anomaly which is quite inexplicable, except on the assumption of an original long *aa*. The development of the word is clearly *ce-aas, ce-òòs, chòòs, chóóz*. This seems to be what Rask meant by his accentuating *eá*, which Grimm also adopted, although Grimm does not seem to have attached any idea of lengthening to the accent.

The development of *eaa* out of *au* is one of the most difficult questions in Teutonic philology. All the explanations hitherto given are utterly unsatisfactory, and I will not waste time in criticising them, but rather state what I consider to be the only tenable theory, which, as far as I know, has never been made public, although I was glad to learn from Professor Kern, of Leiden, that it had suggested itself to him also. The explanation we propose is simply this. *au* first became *aa*, as in Frisian. This *aa* followed the short *a* and became *ææ*. The *ææ* was then resolved into *eaa* or *æaa*. We must suppose that these changes took place before *ai* became *aa*: otherwise there would have been a confusion between *aa*=*au* and *aa*=*ai*. There are, of course, certain difficulties still remaining. The development of a diphthong with one of its elements long is anomalous, and we would expect the diphthongization of the hypothetical *ææ* to take place, like that of short *æ*, only before certain consonants. It is, however, quite possible that the diphthongization of long *ææ* was much earlier than that of short *æ*, and that the two phenomena are therefore independent. If so, *ææ* may at first have developed into simple *ea* and the lengthening of the *a* may have been a secondary process.

EOO

Answers to original *iu*, as in *deop*=Gothic *diup*. There can be no doubt that this *eo*=*iu* was distinct from the *eo*=*é*, and every analogy would lead us to suppose that the difference was one of quantity. Positive confirmation is afforded by the English *chuuz*, which points as clearly to an Old English *ceóósan* as *chóóz* does to a *ceaas*. The Icelandic *ióó*, as in *kióósa* (Modern *kjousa*), shows the same anomalous lengthening of the second element.

There is some uncertainty about the first elements of these diphthongs. Some clue is however afforded by the interchange of *e* with *i* in *eo* and *eoo*, which never happens with *ea* and *eaa*: we often find such forms as *iorðe* for *eorðe*, but never *hiard* for *heard*. The inference clearly is that in *eó* and *eoo* the initial vowel was closer and higher than in *ea*, *eaa*, probably through the assimilative influence of the second element. The diphthongs are then strictly *éó*, *éóó*, *èa*, *èaa* (or possibly *æa*, *æaa*).

For the sake of comparison, I append a table giving Mr. Ellis's results (Early English Pronunciation, p. 534) together

LETTERS.	ELLIS.	SWEET.	LETTERS.	ELLIS.	SWEET.
a	*a*, ɑ	*a*	ā	*aa*	*aa*
æ	æ	æ	ǣ	ææ	EE
ò	o	ɔ	ē	ee	*ee*
i	*i*	i	ī	ii	ii
è	e	E	ō	oo	*oo*
é	e	*e*	ū	uu	uu
u	u, *u*?	u	ȳ	yy, ii	II
ó	o	*o*	ea	ea, e*á*	E*á* (æ*a* ?)
y	y, *i*	I	eo	eo, eó	*eó*
			eā	ea, e*á*	E*áá*
			eō	eo, eó	*eóó*

with my own, both in palæotype. It will be observed that Mr. Ellis (like all his predecessors) confounds the two short *e*s and *o*s, which I have carefully distinguished. He is also not clear as to the distinction between *ea*, *eo*, and *eā*, *eō*. Otherwise our results approximate very closely.

MIDDLE ENGLISH PERIOD.

ORTHOGRAPHY.

Some important revolutions in orthography took place during the transition from the Old to the Middle period—most of them the result of French influence.

There are many instances of French influence on the consonant notation: in the vowels two cases require special notice, these are the use of *u* for the Old English *y*, and of *ou* for the Old English *uu*. The explanation of the former change must be sought in the fact that *y* in the Middle period lost its original value, and became confused with *i*, while in the beginning of words it assumed its present consonantal value. The result was that the old sound of *y* was left without a symbol, and the want was supplied, imperfectly enough, by adopting the French representation of the sound, which was *u*. But *u* was further employed, also in imitation of French usage, to represent the voiced sound of the Old E. *f*, so that *u*, which still retained its original pronunciation in many cases, stood for three distinct sounds. In course of time the short *y*-sound disappeared more and more, and at the same time a large number of long *y*s were introduced in words taken from the French, which were all written with *u* (*nature*, etc.). To remedy the consequent confusion between *u*=*yy* and *u*=*uu* (*hus*, etc.), the French *ou* was introduced as the representation of the latter sound, so that *natyyre* and *huus* were distinguished in writing as *nature* and *hous*. For the details of the change of *u* into *ou* I must refer to Mr. Ellis's Early English Pronunciation, where the subject is treated at great length.

These changes are important, as showing that the Middle

English scribes were not at all biassed by traditions of the earlier orthography, and therefore that their testimony can be unhesitatingly accepted, as far as it goes.

We may now turn to the actual sound-changes, beginning with the most important and characteristic of them all, which I will call

Vowel-levelling.

In the Transition period (Semi-Saxon) we are confronted by the curious and apparently inexplicable phenomenon of a language ignoring, as it were, the changes of an earlier period, and returning to the original sounds. Such is at least the case with the Old English modifications of *a* and *é*: where Old English has *æ*, *ea* or *eo*, Middle English has the unmodified *a* and *e*. Compare *glæd*, *heard*, *seofon*, with the Middle English *glad*, *hard*, *seven*.

Such a change as that of *glæd* into *glad* is doubly anomalous, both as being a return to a pronunciation older than that of the oldest extant documents before the Conquest, and also as a change from a weak front to a strong back vowel. It is, in short, inexplicable, if considered as an ordinary organic sound-change. The explanation must be sought among the inorganic sound-changes, due to some purely external cause.

One of the most unmistakable of these inorganic sound-changes is one which may be called levelling. The whole history of English inflection is mainly one of levelling. Thus, in Old English we find the plural formed in a great variety of ways, sometimes in *as*, sometimes in *an*, sometimes with different vowels, and sometimes without any change at all. In Modern English we have only the first, which, originally restricted to a limited number of masculine substantives, is now extended to all substantives without distinction. It would evidently be absurd to attempt to explain these changes as organic, to adduce, for instance, the change of the Old English plural *heortan* into the Modern *harts* as a case of *n* becoming *s*. They are clearly due to external causes, and are simply the result of that tendency to get rid of useless complexity which characterizes the more advanced stages of language: instead of indicating plurality by a variety of terminations, some of which were of a very vague and indistinct character, the later language selected that termination which seemed the most distinctive, and discarded the rest.

We can now understand how men who were engaged every day of their lives in this levelling process, whose language was being broken up and reconstructed with unexampled rapidity —we can understand how those who spoke the Transition English of the twelfth century came unconsciously to regard the alternation of *æ* and *a* in such words as *dæg*, *dagas*, as an unnecessary piece of discrimination, comparable to that involved in the use of a large number of plural terminations. And so the indistinct *æ*—so liable to be confounded with è—was discarded, and the clear sounding *a* was made the sole representative of the older *a* and *æ*.

When this process of levelling had once begun, it is easy to see how *ea* and *eo* also came to be regarded as superfluous modifications of *a* and *e*, and were therefore in like manner discarded. As we shall see hereafter, *eaa* and *eoo* (=original *au* and *iu*) were simplified into *èè* and *éé* respectively; it is, therefore, probable that *ea* and *eo* themselves were first simplified into *è* and *é*. It is further probable that the first sound of the *è*=*ea* was identical with that of the Old English *æ*. *heard* would, therefore, become *hærd*, whose *æ* would naturally follow the other *æ*s, and become *a*, giving the Middle English *hard*. The three spellings *heard*, *hærd*, and *hard* are to be found constantly interchanging in Laȝamon and other writers of the period.

Whatever may be the explanation of the fact, there can be no doubt that the Old English *æ*, *ea*, *eo*, were lost in the Middle period, and that the mysterious connection between the Old English *æ* and the Modern sound in such a word as *mæn* (written *man*) imagined by some philologists, must be given up: the two *æ*s are quite independent developments, even when they occur in the same words, as in *ðæt*, *sæt*, *sæd*, *æppel*. Mr. Ellis has shown that up to the seventeenth century these words were pronounced *ðat*, *sat*, *sad*, *apl*, even in the court dialect, and the sound *æ* is unknown up to the present day in most of our dialects.

Before investigating the sound-changes of the Middle period in detail, it will be necessary to state the general laws which govern the remarkable qualitative divergence of long and short vowels in the later Teutonic languages. If it can once be shown that all the Teutonic languages follow the same general laws, it is but reasonable to suppose that the same laws will be found valid in the case of Middle English also. We shall have still less hesitation in applying these laws to the elucidation of the Middle English sound-changes, when we consider that the English of the thirteenth century was really as much in advance of its contemporaries as Modern English is of its, and that Middle English is practically on a level with Dutch and the other living Teutonic languages. German, indeed, is in many respects much more archaic than Middle English, and may be said to stand to it in almost the same relation as Old English does.

I propose, therefore, to give an impartial classification of the principal changes that have taken place in the living Teutonic languages, beginning with the long vowels.

A. Long Vowels.

1) Back to round (p. 11). Long *a*, whatever its origin, has in all the Teutonic languages except German and Dutch been rounded. Even German and Dutch show the same change in many of their dialects, which give long *a* the sound of the low-back-narrow-round (English *fall*). This is also the Swedish and Danish sound, the only difference being that the Scandinavian vowel is pronounced with greater lip narrowing, so that its sound approximates to that of the regular close *ó* (the "mid" vowel).

2) Front-round to unrounded (page 11). Exemplified in the familiar German change of *œ* and *y* into *é* and *i*, as in *shéén* and *kiin* for *shœœn* and *kyyn*. In Modern Icelandic *œœ* became first unrounded, and the resulting *ee* ran

II.

TEUTONIC LONG VOWELS.[1]

	AA	II	OO		UU		AI	AU	IU
	1	2	3	4	5	6	7	8	9
1 Gothic	*ded*	*wein*	*god*	—	*hus*	—	*stain*	*draum*	*diup*
2 Old High German	*tāt*	*wīn*	*guot*	*gruoni*	*hūs*	*hūsir*	*stain* *stein*	*traum* *troum*	*tiuf*
3 Modern High German	taat	wain	guut	gryyn	haus	hayzer	shtain	traum	tiif
4 Old Saxon	*dad*	*win*	*god*	*groni*	*hus*	—	*sten*	*drom*	*diop*
5 Dutch	daat	wèin	ghut	ghrun	hœys zyyr	—	stéén	dróóm	dip
6 Old Icelandic	*dāð*	*wīn*	*gṓð*	*grǣn*	*hūs*	*kȳr*	*stèin*	*draum*	*diūp* *siōn*
7 Modern Icelandic	dauð	viin	góuð	grain	huus	kiir	stéin	drœim	djuup sjóun
8 Swedish	dòòd	viin	góód	grœœn	h*uu*s[2]	lyytə	stéén	drœm	dj*uu*p syyn
9 Danish	dòòð	viin	góóð	grœn	huus	lyyðə	stéén	drœm	dyyb syyn
10 Old English	*dæd*	*win*	*god*	*grene*	*hus*	*cȳ*	*stan*	*dream* (=eaa)	*deop* (=cóó)
11 Middle English	*deed* (=éé)	*wiin*	*good* (=óó)	*green* (=éé)	*hous(e)* (=uu)	*kye*	*ston(e)* (=òò)	*dream* (=èè)	*deep* (=éé)
12 Modern English	ddii	wain	gud	griin	haus	kai	stóun	driim	diip

[1] In this and the following table the actual spelling (not the theoretical pronunciation) of the dead languages is given in italics; the modern forms are written phonetically.

[2] The italics indicate the peculiar Swedish *u*—intermediate to *u* and *y*.

together with the regular *èè*, and, like it, was diphthongized into *ai*, so that the Old Icelandic *bœœkr* is now disguised under the form of *baikər*. The same change took place in Old English, only it was not carried so far: the *bœœk* (written *boec* or *beoc*, p. 23) of the oldest period appears in the later MSS. as *bec* (=*béék*). In Middle English we have the unrounding of *y* into *i*, *cyning* becoming *cing*.

3) Low to mid. Modern English, as will be shown hereafter, affords two unmistakable instances of this change. It is also certain that the German *óó* from *au* was originally "low," for in the Oldest High German such words as *lóós* (=*laus*) are frequently written *laos*. Similar evidence can be adduced in the case of the corresponding Dutch *óó*. The *ee* from *ai* has in like manner passed through the low to the mid stage in German and Dutch.

4) Mid to high. Of this change, again, Modern English affords illustrations, whose consideration must be deferred. Original *óó* has in nearly all the Teutonic languages been raised from the mid position it still preserves in Swedish and Danish (although even here with a slight labial modification in the direction of *u*) to the high one of *u*.

5) High to diphthong. With the high position the extreme is reached, as far as position is concerned. We find, accordingly, that the two high vowels *ii* and *uu* either remain unchanged, which is the case in the Scandinavian languages, or else undergo various modifications in the direction of *ai* and *au*. As there can be no question that Middle English agreed with the Scandinavian languages in retaining long *i* and *u* unchanged, the consideration of their diphthongization may be deferred till we come to the Modern period, to which belongs also the development of the diphthong *iu* out of *yy*.

6) Besides these regular modifications of the two high vowels, there are isolated diphthongizations of other vowels.

a) *óó* to *ou*. In Icelandic *gouð* for the older *góóð*, and Modern English *stóun* for *stóón*.

b) *éé* to *éi*. In the Modern English *téik* for *téék*.

c) *óó* to *uo*. In the Old German *guot* for *góót*, still preserved in South German in the shape of *guət*.

d) *òò* to *au*. In Icelandic, where original *aa* passed through the stage of simple rounding (*òò*), and was then resolved into *au*, *laata* (let) becoming first *lòòta* and then *lauta*.

e) *èè* to *ai*. The *i*-umlaut of *aa* has in the same way been resolved into *ai* in Modern Icelandic, so that *rèèri* (written *væri*) is now *rairi*.

7) Back to front. Exemplified in the Dutch *zyyr* for *zuur*.

B. Short Vowels.

1) Round to unrounded. In Icelandic, English, and some German dialects *y* has been unrounded into *i*. The same is the case with short *œ* in German. In Modern English we have, lastly, a very anomalous case of unrounding of the back vowel *u*, *but* becoming *bət*.

2) Back to front. Short *u* has in Icelandic and Dutch been changed into a front vowel—the high-front-wide-round in Icelandic, the low-front-narrow-round (or its imitation, the mid-mixed-narrow) in Dutch. The open *ò* in Icelandic (the *u*-umlaut of *a*) has changed into *œ* (the mid-front-wide-round), *mònnum* becoming *mœnnym*. Short *a* has, lastly, been changed into the low-front-wide (*æ*) in a few English dialects—including the literary English.

3) Mid to low. The two mid vowels *é* and *ó* have in all the Teutonic languages been brought down to the low position, so that the old distinction between *è* and *é* has been lost everywhere, except, perhaps, in some German dialects: compare Old English *ènde*, *hélpan*, with the Modern levellings *ènd*, *hèlp*.

2) High to mid. As a general rule the high vowels *i* and *u* have retained their positions, but in Dutch the short *i* is now represented by the mid-front-wide, and the short *u* by *ó* (the mid-narrow), thus taking the place of original short *o*, which, as in the other languages, has been lowered to *ò* (the low-wide): compare *stòk* with *bók* (=*buk*). The peculiar Modern English *u* in *but* (*bət*) seems also to be a case of lowering from high to mid.

III.

TEUTONIC SHORT VOWELS

	A				I				U				
	1	2	3	4	5	6	7		8	9	10	11	12
1 Gothic	*mann*	*namo* *wakan*	*andi-*	*nati* *mati-*	*winnan*	*witan*	*drigkan* *hilpan*	*stilan*	*sunno*	*sunru*	*ufta*	*hul*	*fulljan*
2 Old Icel.	*mann* *mònnum*	*vaka*	*èndi*	*nèt*	*vinna*	*vita*	*drékka*	*stéla*	*sunna*	*sumar*	*opt*	*hól*	*fylla*
3 Mod. Icel.	man mœnnym	vaaka	èndi	nèèt	vinna[1]	viita	drèkka	stèèla	synna	syymar	òft	hòòl	fidla *Sw.* fylla
4 Old Engl.	*mann* *heard* *lòng*	*nama*	*ènde*	*mète*	*winnan*	*witan*	*hélpan* *heofon*	*stéla*	*sunne*	*sumor*	*óft*	*hól*	*fyllan*
5 Mid. Engl.	*man* *hard* *long* (=ò)	*name* (=naam)	*end* (=è)	*meat* (=èè)	*win*	*wit*	*help* *heven* (=è)	*steal* (=èè)	*sun*	*summer* (=sumer)	*oft* (=ò)	*hole* (=hòòl)	*fill*
6 Mod. Engl.	mænn haəd lòng	néim	ènd	miit	winn	wit	hèlp hèvən	stiil	sən	səmər	òft	hóul	fil

[1] Italics indicate wide vowels.

The only exception to this general lowering tendency is the frequent shifting of the *a* from the low to the mid position, which is very common in all the languages. The low sound is still preserved in South Scotch, Dutch, and many German dialects, and may be heard in some of the London dialects, where, however, it is probably quite a modern development.

We have, lastly, to consider the important distinction of narrow and wide. Here, also, short and long vowels pursue opposite courses, the general rule being that long vowels remain or become narrow, short vowels wide. These tendencies are at once apparent on comparing any pairs of long and short vowels in the more advanced Teutonic languages, in fact in all of them more or less, except German.

The principle has been carried out with such strictness in the case of the long vowels that, with the single exception of *aa*, all originally long vowels are now narrow in the Teutonic languages. The cause of this exceptional widening of *aa* has already been explained (page 28) as the result of the greater energy required in the formation of the narrow sound.

The short vowels are less consistent. In the first place, some of the languages show the tendency to widening either not at all, or else only partially. In South German all the short vowels are still narrow, including even the *a* (p. 28). In Danish and Swedish short *i* is sometimes narrow, sometimes wide, according to the nature of the following consonant.

The languages in which the principle is most strictly carried out are Icelandic and English. The only exceptions are the *è*, which is narrow in both languages, and the English *ɔ* in *bɔt* (mid-back-narrow). The retention of the narrow *è* in all the Teutonic languages is a very curious phenomenon: it is not easy to see why it did not everywhere weaken into the wide *æ*, which it actually has done in the Dutch *kærk* for *kèrk* and several other words, and also in the South Scotch dialect of Teviotdale, where the English distinction of *mæn*, *mèn*, is represented by *man*, *mæn*.

The change of the low-narrow *è* into the mid-wide is, on the other hand, very common, and in many of the languages, as, for instance, English, the two sounds seem to be used almost indiscriminately. This change is, no doubt, a purely imitative one: the change from the low-narrow to the mid-wide must have been direct. To assume that the low-narrow was first widened, and then raised to the mid position, would be to ignore the fundamental laws of short vowel change.

We now see how complete the divergence is between long and short vowels. Long vowels contract both the pharyngal and the oral passage as much as possible, the former by "narrowing," the latter by raising the tongue and contracting the lips; short vowels pursue the very opposite course; high long vowels are never lowered, except partially by diphthongization; high short vowels are never diphthongized, but simply lowered.

Quantity

The general principles on which quantitative changes in the Teutonic languages depend are these:

1) unaccented vowels are shortened, accented vowels are lengthened or shortened under certain conditions, which are:
2) before a single consonant they are lengthened.
3) before double or combined consonants they are shortened.

The result of all these changes, if carried out strictly, would be to eliminate all short accented syllables altogether, and this is actually the case in Modern Icelandic, at least in polysyllables—either the vowel itself is long, or else, if it is short, the syllable is made long by a double consonant. In the other languages, however, the double consonants have been simplified, so that a large number of short accented syllables has been formed: compare Icelandic *vinna* with Danish *vinə* (written *vinde*) and English *winər*, *wining*, German *gəwinən*. This simplification of double consonants has taken place in Icelandic also in the case of monosyllables such as *man* (written *mann*).

An important result of the simplification is the use of double consonants as a purely graphic expedient to denote the shortness of the preceding vowel. The double *m*, for instance, in *summer*, is simply a way of showing that the original shortness of the *u* has been preserved.

In Icelandic the lengthening of short vowels has been carried out with perfect consistency, but in the other languages there are many exceptions. Thus in Dutch all monosyllables preserve their shortness: compare *vat, lòt,* with the plurals *vaatən, lóótən.* The retention of original short quantity before single consonants is also very frequent in Modern, and consequently also in Middle English.

The chief cases in which Modern English preserves the Old English short quantity are these.

In the first place the high vowels *i(y), u* are not lengthened: compare *wit* from *witan* with *iit* from *etan, sən* from *sunu* and *cəm* from *cuman* with *néim* from *nama.* Exceptions, such as *aivi* from *ifig*, do occur, but they are very few.

English, like Dutch, shows a strong tendency to preserve short quantity in monosyllables, although there are many cases of lengthening. Nevertheless, it may safely be said that the great majority of Old English monosyllables preserve their short quantity in Modern English. Examples are: *swon* (from *swan*), *þæch* (*þæc*), *bæc (bæc), sæd (sæd), lot (hlot), god (god), woz (wæs).* Examples of lengthening are *géiv (geaf), céim (cam), éit (æt), géit (geat), yóuc (geoc).* The lengthened vowels in the adjectives *téim* and *léit* may perhaps have arisen from the definite forms *tama, lata.*

Dissyllables ending in a vowel, or the infinitival *an*, are almost always lengthened: *nama, scamu, flotian, brecan,* become *néim, shéim, flóut, bréic.* But there are exceptions: *dropa* becomes *drop*, and *hafan* (*=habban*) becomes *hæv*, contrasting with the regular *behéiv* (from *behabban*).

But besides these isolated irregularities, there is a whole class of dissyllables which resists the lengthening tendency, namely those which end in a liquid or nasal. Examples are *hæmər* (from *hamor*), *betər* (*bèter*), *sædl* (*sadol*), *əvən* (*ofen*), *botəm* (*botom*). There are, however, several exceptions. In the first place, all the past participles in *o* (except *trodn*) lengthen their vowel: *frouzən*, *chóuzən*, *clóuvən*, etc. There are also others, such as *iivən* (*efen*), *óuvər* (*ofer*), *eicər* (*æcer*), etc.

In applying these deductions to Middle English we are confronted by a formidable difficulty. The Midland writer Orm, as is well known, indicates short vowel quantity by doubling the following consonant. If, then, we find Orm in the thirteenth century writing always *witenn*, *sune*, not *wittenn*, *sunne*, how can we escape the conclusion that he said *wiiten*, *suune*? If we accept the long vowels for the thirteenth century, we are forced to assume that the original short vowels were first lengthened and then shortened again *before* the diphthongization of *ii* and *uu* into *ei* and *ou*; for, otherwise, we should have had *wait* and *saun* in Modern English. Rather than accept this very improbable hypothesis, it seems safer to reserve any decided conclusion till the difficult question of quantity in the Ormulum has been more fully investigated.

The Modern forms of many words point clearly to their originally long vowels having been shortened in the Middle period. Besides the frequent shortening before two consonants, which will be considered hereafter, there are some cases before single consonants. Long *ii* is, as might be expected, often shortened, as in *stif*, *dich*, and in other words where it stands for various other O.E. long vowels, such as *sili*=O.E. *gesǣlig* and *chil*=*cēle*. Examples of other vowels are *ten*=O.E. *ten*, *wet*=*wǣt*, *let*=*lǣtan*, *lēt*. In *ever*=*ǣver* =*æfre*, the shortening may be ascribed to the liquid in the following syllable.

Close and Open EE and OO in Middle English.

We can now enter on the important question of the distinction between close and open *ee* and *oo* in Middle English.

Mr. Ellis, relying on the fact that Chaucer rhymes all the *ees* and *oos* together without distinction, comes to the conclusion that there was only one sound, but he does not explain how the modern distinctions arose, or how it is that they correspond to distinctions in Old English. If *too* and *taa* are distinct in Old English, and are separated in the form of *tuu* and *too* in Modern English also, it is not easy to see how they could have been confounded in the Middle period. This view was vaguely indicated many years ago by Rapp, and has been recently revived by Dr. Weymouth, who is, however, clearly wrong in assuming that the Middle English sounds were identical with the Modern ones.

As the whole question offers considerable difficulties of detail, I propose to examine it as impartially as possible, utilizing all the evidence that is afforded by the graphic forms, by the general laws of change just stated, by the pronunciation of the sixteenth century, as investigated by Mr. Ellis, and by the pronunciation of the present day. I begin with the *oo*s, as offering less difficulty than the *ee*s.

Beginning, then, with the *oo*s, we find that Middle English *oo* corresponds to three distinct sounds in Old English,

1) to *óó:* too, O.E. tóó (*too*),

2) to *aa:* too, O.E. taa (*toe*),

3) to *ó* short: hool, O.E. hól (*hole*).

Of these three *oo*s the two first are kept quite distinct in the present Modern English, original *óó* being now pronounced *uu*, while *oo* from *aa* is now *óó* or *óu*. The natural inference that the two sounds were also kept distinct in the Middle period is fully confirmed by the graphic evidence, for in the earlier writings the *oo* from *aa* is often spelt *oa*, as in *oaðe*= O.E. *aaðe* (Laȝamon), *noan*=*naan* (Procl. of H. III.), *moare* =*maare* (Procl. and A. Riwle), *þoa*=*þaa* (A. Riwle). The clear inference is that the *oo* from *aa* was pronounced with a sound intermediate to *oo* and *aa*, and consequently that original *oo* still retained its Old English sound.

The *oo* of *hool*, arising from original short *ó*, is in the present pronunciation represented by the same vowel as the *oo* from *aa:* it is therefore highly probable that it had in Middle English the same sound as the *oo* from *aa*, namely the more open one.

We may now examine the question from the comparative point of view, and see whether the results harmonize.

The first two *oo*s need not detain us long. We have seen that original *óó* is, as a general rule, either retained without change, or else moved up into the *u*-position. It is quite certain that this change had not taken place in the Middle period: *óó* must, therefore, have been kept unchanged. Again, whenever *aa* has changed, it has been by rounding. It has been already proved that the Old English *aa* cannot well have been any other sound than the low-wide, and this, when rounded, naturally gives the low-back-wide-round.

The *o* of *hol* was almost certainly the mid-narrow sound (p. 30). The tendencies of short vowels are, as we have seen, towards lowering and widening. These modifications, applied to our vowel, give the low-back-wide-round. This vowel was then lengthened, and became identical with the *òò* of *tòò* from *taa*, which, as we have seen, was no other than the low-back-wide-round.

But all long vowels are liable to be narrowed (p. 30), and we find, as a matter of fact, that the *òò* from *aa* is narrow in all the living Teutonic languages which possess it. It is, therefore, not only possible, but extremely probable that the *òò* soon became narrow in Middle English also: *tòò* and *hòòl* would therefore have the sound of the Modern English words which are written *taw* and *haul*.

We may now turn to the *ees*. In the present English all the *ees* are levelled under *ii*, but Mr. Ellis's researches have proved that in the sixteenth century a distinction parallel to that of the two *oos* was still kept up, some of the Middle English *ees* being pronounced *ee*, some *ii*, those words which are now written with *ea* (such as *sea*) having the *ee*-sound, while *ee* (as in *see*) had the *ii*-sound. The analogy of the *oos* leads us to suppose that the sixteenth century *ees* correspond to Middle English *èès*, and the *iis* to *éés*. I will now give an example of the different *ees*, with the original Old English forms, together with those of the sixteenth century and the Middle English forms indicated by them, adding the present English spelling, which is, of course, nothing but a dead tradition of the sixteenth and seventeenth centuries pronunciation.

TENTH CENT.	FOURTEENTH CENT.	SIXTEENTH CENT.	NINETEENTH CENT.
sǣ	sèè	séé	sii (*sea*)
dǣd	dééd	diid	diid (*deed*)
dreām	drèèm	dréém	driim (*dream*)
grēne	gréén	griin	griin (*green*).
deōp	déép	diip	diip (*deep*)
mète	mète / mèèt	méét	miit (*meat*)
stélan	stèlan / stèèl	stéél	stiil (*steal*)

Reserving for the present the apparently anomalous *éé* of *dééd*, the other changes, after what has been said on the *oo*s, call for only a few remarks.

Old English *ǣ* and *ē* remain unchanged in the Middle period. Of the two diphthongs *eā*, when simplified, naturally takes the low position of its principal element (the *ā*), and *eō*, as naturally, takes the mid position of its *ō*. *é*, following the usual tendencies of short vowels, is lowered, and the two short *e*s are consequently levelled under the common form è, which is afterwards lengthened. All the vowels either remain or become narrow.

An important class of apparent exceptions is exemplified in *dǣd*, whose *ǣ* is represented in Middle English not by *èè*, as would be expected, but by *éé*. An examination of these anomalous *ǣ*s soon reveals the fact that they correspond not to Gothic and general Teutonic *ai*, but to Gothic *ē*, general Teutonic *ā* (Gothic *dēds*, Old High German *tāt*). This is clearly one of the many cases in which the explanation of later English forms must be sought not in the literary West-Saxon, but rather in the Mercian dialect, in which the distinction between *éé*=original *aa* and *èè*=*ai* was still kept up. In short, the Middle English *dééd* is descended not from *dǣd*, but from *dēd*. Traces of this older *éé* have been preserved in West-Saxon also, not only in such words as *wēn* and *cwēn*, but also in the *rēd* of the name *Ælfrēd*, which is never written *ræd*—the regular form of the substantive *rǣd*, when it stands alone.

Unaccented E.

Middle English, like the majority of the living Teutonic languages, levels all the Old English unaccented vowels under *e*: compare Old E. *caru*, *nama*, *gifan*, with the Middle forms *care*, *name*, *given*. The sound of this *e* in Modern German, Swedish, Danish, and Dutch, is the mid-mixed-narrow, although, as we have seen (p. 30), there are traces of an older front sound, which we have theoretically assigned to the Old English final *e*. When we consider that the Middle English *e* in the fourteenth century was on the verge of extinction, we cannot well claim for it so archaic a sound as in Old English, and the analogy of the modern languages points clearly to some mixed vowel. Nor is graphic evidence wanting. The confusion and uncertainty of usage in the Middle English orthography shows clearly that the scribes were not satisfied with the letter *e* as a representative of the sound of unaccented *e*. In Wiclif's Bible, for instance, we find, besides the regular *ende*, *synnes*, such spellings as *mannis*, *mannys*, *fadir*, *opyn*, *writun*, *locustus*, constantly occurring. It is not improbable that the *u* is intended for the French *u* (=*y*), and that this spelling is an attempt to represent the obscure sound of the mid-mixed, which, like all the mixed vowels, has a distinctly *labial* effect on the ear (p. 16).

Diphthongs. (*See also* p. 148.)

Middle English, while simplifying, as we have seen, the Old English diphthongs, developed some new ones of its own. All the Middle English diphthongs, with the exception of those in words taken from Norse and French, arose from weakening of the consonants *g* and *w*, by which *g* passed through *gh* (as in German *sagen*) into *i* or *u*, and *w* into *u*. The most important of these diphthongs are *ai*, *au*, *eu*, and *ou*.

ai arises from O.E. *ag* (*æg*), *ég*, *ѐg*, *ēg*, *ǣg*: *dai* (from *dæg*), *wai* (*wég*), *sai* (*sѐcgan*), *hai* (*hēg*), *clai* (*clǣg*).

au arises from O.E. *aw*, *ag*: *clau* (*clawu*), *drau* (*dragan*).

eu arises from O.E. *iw*, *īw*, *ǣw*, *eāw*, *eōw*: *neu* (*niwe*), *speu* (*spīwan*), *leud* (*lǣwed*), *heu* (*heāwan*), *cneu* (*cneōw*).

ou (*òòu*, *óóu*) arises from O.E. *āw*, *ōw*: *sòòu* (*sāwan*), *blóóu* (*blōwan*).

The development of *ai* from *èi* (*sai*=*sèi*=*sècgan*) is paralleled by the Danish pronunciation of *ei* (as in *vei*=*veg*) as *ai*, and is probably the result of an attempt to bring out the diphthongic character of the combination more clearly. There are, however, traces of original *ei* even in the Modern period, in such words as *eiht*, *eiðer*=*eahta*, *ægðer*.

It will be observed that *ag* sometimes becomes *ai*, sometimes *au*. The general rule is that *ag* final or before a consonant becomes *ai*, while, if followed by the back vowels *a* or *u*, the diphthong *au* is developed. Thus, *dag* (*dæg*), *tagl* (*tægl*), *magn* (*mægen*), become *dai*, *tail*, *main*, while *dragan*, *sagu*, become *drau*, *sau*. We have, however, *sau* from *sage*.

The change of *i* into *eu* in the combination *iu*, and the levelling of the quantities of *iw*, *īw*, etc., must be noticed, although the cause is not apparent.

That the *oou*-diphthongs preserved the long quantity of their first elements is clear from the accounts of the sixteenth century phoneticians; the separation of *òòu* and *óóu* is theoretical.

In the combinations *ig* and *ug* the consonant is naturally absorbed by the vowel, the result being simply a long vowel: *lii* (*licgan*), *uul* (*ugle*).

Consonant Influence.

Quantity. Short vowels are lengthened before liquids and nasals followed by a voice stop—before *ld*, *nd*, *mb* (often also before *rd* and a few other *r*-combinations). Thus Old English *wilde*, *findan*, *climban*, become *wiild*, *fiind*, *cliimb*, the length of whose vowels is shown by the modern forms *waild*, *faind*, *claim*. Exceptions can be explained on the same principle as the other cases of the abnormal retention of original short quantity, namely, by the presence of a liquid in the second syllable; hence *hinder*, *wunder*, *timber*, not *hiinder*, etc.

Quality. *a* before *ld* is rounded into *ò*, and then, in accordance with the rule just stated, lengthened, so that the Old English *sealde* passes through *salde* into *sòlde*, and finally becomes *sòòlde*, whence the Modern *sóóld*.

The rounding of short *a* before nasals, which almost disappeared towards the end of the Old English period, at least in West-Saxon, crops up again in Middle English. An examination of the present forms gives the following rules for the occurrence of *ò*=*a* before nasals. Most of the cases of rounding are before *ng*, the general rule being that while verb preterites keep *a*, all other words have *ò*. Thus we have the substantive *song*, but the preterite *sang*. Exceptions are *hang* and *fang*, which should regularly be *hong*, *fong*. Rounding before *n* and *m* is exceptional: the only examples are *on*, *bond*, *from*, *wóómb*, *còòmb*.

Initial *w* influences the following vowel in various ways. Sometimes it assimilates *i* into *u*, which then absorbs the *w* itself, as in *such*=*swich*=O.E. *swilc*. Occasionally it draws up *òò* to the *óó*-position, as in *twóó* for *twòò*, *wóómb* for *wòòmb*, contrasting with the regular *wòò*, *wòòd* (O.E. *wā*, *wād*). Hence, by the regular changes, the Modern *twuu*, *tuu*, *wuum(b)*, *wóó*, *wóód*.

We may now sum up briefly the changes of the Middle period.

a is preserved, except before *ld*, where it is rounded, and *æ* and *ea* are levelled under it.

è and *é*, together with *eo*, are levelled under *è*.

y is confounded with *i*, which remains unchanged, except that it was probably widened.

ó becomes *ò*, and *ò* is kept unchanged.

u remains, although probably widened.

a, *è*, and *ò* are often lengthened, giving *aa*, *èè* and *òò*. It will be observed that the Old English *é* and *ó* are not lengthened into *éé* and *óó*, but pass through *è* and *ò* into *èè* and *òò*.

Of the long vowels *ǣ*, *ē*, *ī*, *ō*, *ū* remain unchanged.

ȳ becomes *ii*.

ā becomes *òò*.

Of the diphthongs *eă* becomes *èè*, *eŏ* becomes *éé*.

New diphthongs are developed by the weakening of *g* and *w*.

Unaccented vowels are levelled under *ə*.

Short vowels are often lengthened before liquids followed by voice stops.

MODERN PERIOD.

Loss of final E.

The loss of final *e* in English is one of the many instances of how the whole grammatical structure of a language may be subverted by purely phonetic changes, for it may safely be said that the loss of final *e* in Modern English is almost equivalent to loss of inflexion altogether. Middle English, although much reduced, was still distinctly an inflexional language, as much so at least as Modern Danish or Swedish: its verbs had infinitive and plural endings, and its adjectives still retained some of their old inflexions, including the peculiarly Teutonic distinction of definite and indefinite. In Modern English all this is lost: not only is the distinction of definite and indefinite lost, but our adjectives have become absolutely indeclinable, and the whole spirit of English is now so different from that of the other Teutonic languages, that their most familiar distinctions are quite strange to us, and can only be acquired with considerable difficulty.

The loss of final *e* marks off English sharply and distinctly from the cognate languages, in all of which it is strictly preserved. Those who have such difficulty in admitting, even after the clearest evidence, that Chaucer may possibly have pronounced the final *e*, should try to realize to themselves the fact that the loss of final *e* is really quite an exceptional and anomalous phenomenon: instead of being surprised at Chaucer still retaining it, they should rather be surprised at its loss at so early a period as the fifteenth century, while preserved to the present day in all the cognate languages.

An important result of the loss of final *e* was to prevent change in other directions: we shall find that the Middle English sounds were preserved almost unchanged long after its disappearance. Mr. Ellis's researches have shown that the most characteristic features of Middle English, as, for instance, *ii* and *uu*, were preserved some way into the sixteenth century; others, such as the old *ai* and *au*, still later.

But the tendency to change soon begins to manifest itself, and by the beginning of the seventeenth century we find many important changes either completed, or else in partial operation. During the latter half of the seventeenth century the whole phonetic structure of the language may be said to have been revolutionized. Some slight further changes took place during the first half of the eighteenth century, and by the middle of the century the language finally settled down into nearly its present state. We may, therefore, distinguish roughly five periods of Modern English.

1) the *Earliest* (1450–1500 or rather later), which preserves the sounds of the Middle period unchanged, except that it throws off the final *e*. I propose, therefore, for the sake of convenience, to cite the Middle English forms in this Earliest Modern English, which is really equivalent to Latest Middle English.

2) the *Early* (1550–1650), in which the Middle sounds were distinctly modified, *ii* and *uu* being diphthongized, and *éé* and *óó* moved up to the high positions of *ii* and *uu*, *èè* and *òò* being moved into the vacant mid positions.

3) the *Transition* period (1650–1700), characterized by very important and sweeping changes, such as the simplification of the Middle diphthongs *ai* and *au*, the fronting of *a* and *aa* into *æ*, *ææ*, and the development of the peculiarly English *ə* from *u*.

4) the *Late* period (1700 onwards), in which the long vowels of the Transition period undergo a process of lingual narrowing, *ææ* passing through *èè* into *éé*, while *éé* itself becomes *ii*.

5) the *Latest* period, remarkable for its excessive tendency

to diphthongization, especially in the case of *éé* and *óó*, which are in the present generation almost always *éi* and *óu*.

It is probable that many of the distinctive features of this period existed already in the previous period, either as individual peculiarities or as vulgarisms. It is certain that in the present generation many new pronunciations, which are really very widely distributed, are entirely ignored, or else denounced as vulgarisms, even by the people who employ them habitually. These unrecognized pronunciations are of two kinds, 1) those which, though ignored by every one, are in universal use, and 2) those which appear only sporadically in educated speech, although many of them are firmly established in the language of the populace. As these pronunciations are of great philological importance, as showing us the changes of sound in active operation, and as they have been hitherto quite ignored by phoneticians, I propose to treat of them hereafter as fully as my imperfect observations will allow.

EARLY MODERN PERIOD.

a, aa. Mr. Ellis's authorities seem to describe a very thin sound of the *a*, although the *æ* of the following period does not seem to have been recognized. I think it very probable that the real sound was that of the present Danish *a* in *mand, mane*, which is the mid-back-wide-forward, the tongue being advanced considerably, while the tip is kept down. When the tongue is in this position, a very slight raising of the middle of it towards the palate converts this forward *a* into *æ*, which it closely resembles in sound.

e, i, o. As these vowels are retained unchanged in the present English, any discussion of their pronunciation in the Early Modern period is superfluous.

u. That *u* still retained its original sound is clear from the statements of the phonetic authorities. Salesbury writes it with his Welsh *w*, as in *bwck=buck*.

y. It is interesting to observe that there are distinct traces of the old short *y* in the Early Modern period. Clear evidence is afforded by a passage of Salesbury, which I think

Mr. Ellis has misunderstood. Salesbury says (E. E. P. pp. 111, 164) that "Welsh *u* soundeth as the vulgar English people sound it in these words of English, *trust*, *bury*, *busy*, *Huberden*." Mr. Ellis thinks that Salesbury means nothing but the wide as opposed to the narrow *i*. It seems improbable that so minute a distinction should have been noticed by Salesbury—still more that, even if he had noticed it, he should have gone out of his way to describe it. Nor do I agree with Mr. Ellis in considering the distinction between the Welsh *u* and the wide *i* as being very slight. My own observations of the Welsh *u*, as pronounced in North Wales, fully confirm Mr. Bell's identification of it with the high-mixed-wide vowel (although it seems to be narrow when long), which Mr. Ellis also adopts, but the sound seems to me to be as distinct from *i* as the unaccented German *e* (the mid-mixed-narrow) is from *é* (the mid-front), and to be much more like *y* than *i* (p. 16). I think Mr. Ellis has been led astray by Mr. Bell's identification of the unaccented *e* in *fishes*, etc., with this high-mixed vowel, which I believe to be erroneous. Mr. Bell acutely observed that the *e* in *fishes* was not identical with the preceding *i*, and being unable to find a place for it among his front vowels, fell back on the mixed. I find, however, that the real distinction is that the unaccented vowel is the high-front-wide lowered half-way to the mid position, a sound which Dr. Murray recognizes in Scotch, and writes (é).[1]

That the Welsh *u* sounded to Salesbury himself very like *y* is clear from his express statement that the French *u*, the German *ü*, and the Scotch *u*, closely resembled his own *u* (E. E. P. p. 761). If, now, we examine the four English words given by Salesbury, we shall find that the history of all of them points decisively to the *y*-sound. *Bury* and *busy* are in Old English *bebyrgan* and *bysig*, *trust* is the Norse *treysta*, a diphthong which could not well contract into any vowel but *y*, and the first half of *Huberden* is probably the French *Hubert*, which, of course, had the *y*-sound. What

[1] Dialect of the Southern Counties of Scotland, p. 106.

Salesbury's statement amounts to is, therefore, that these three words (for we may pass over the last) were in the sixteenth century pronounced by the vulgar *tryst, byri, byzi.*

Although Salesbury characterizes these pronunciations as vulgar, it is quite clear, from the retention of the French spelling *u*=*y* in all of them up to the present day, that the old pronunciation must have been kept up some way into the Modern period. Whenever we find a word written with *y* in Old English, and with *u* in the present spelling, we may suppose it preserved the *y*-sound in the beginning, at least, of the Modern period. Such words are:

burden (bəədn)...O.E. byrðen..................M.E. burþen, birþen, berþen
bury (beri) ......bebyrgan ....burien, birien, berien
busy (bizi).........bysig......... ....busi, bisi, besi
church (chəəch)...cyrice (early O.E. cirice)...churche, chirche, cherche
much (məch)......mycel (early O.E. micel)...muche(l), michel, mechel, moche
shut (shət) ....scyttan ....schutten, schitten, schetten

There are besides two interesting words in which the *y*-sound is expressed by the digraph *ui*, which are:

build (bild).........O.E. byldan ..................M.E. build, buld, bild, beld
guilt (gilt) ....gylt ....gult, gilt, gelt

The correspondence between the Old, Modern, and Middle forms, the latter (which are taken from Stratmann's Dictionary), with their constant alternation between *u* and *i*, requires little comment. It is quite clear that the ambiguous *u* and *i* were considered unsatisfactory representations of the *y*-sound, and recourse was therefore had to the digraph *ui*, which, as we see, was employed both in the Middle and Modern periods. The forms in *e* point to a previous lowering of the *y* to one of the *æ*-positions. The *o* of *moche* seems to show that there was a spoken, and not merely written form *muche* in the Middle period, with an anomalous change of *y* into *u*.

These words evidently caused considerable embarrassment to the phonetic writers of the Early Modern period, for they had no proper sign for short *y*, and were compelled to identify it with the long French *yy* in *myyz* (written *muse*), or else, if they wished to preserve its quantity, to confound it with short *i*. I will now give the sixteenth century pronunciations of these words, as deduced by Mr. Ellis. I have not made any alteration in his spelling, except in the case of Salesbury's *u*, which I have written *y*, as there seems to me to be no doubt that this was the sound intended by him. I have not thought it necessary to add the authorities, except in the case of Salesbury.

burden: u.
bury: y (Sa.).
busy: y (Sa.).
church: y (Sa.), yy, i, u.
much: i, u? y?
shut: i.
build: yy, ii, i, ei (=Middle E. ii).
guilt: i.

The long *yy* in *chyyrch* is probably a mere inaccuracy of Smith's, for Salesbury writes distinctly *tsurts*, not *tsuurts*, as he would have done had the vowel been long. The *yy* of *byyld* may, on the other hand, be correct, for *y* may very well have been lengthened before *ld*, as *i* is (*wiild*=O.E. *wilde*).

The *us* in these words (except perhaps in *much*) I am inclined to regard as mere pedantry—the attempt to conform the pronunciation to the spelling, of which we have numerous instances in that very pedantic age. Of this artificial *u* for *y* the foreign word *just* is a striking example. This word was certainly never pronounced with *u* in the Middle period, and even at the present day the legitimate descendant of the old *jyst* is still to be heard from all uneducated and many educated speakers in the form of *jist*. Yet we find the artificial *u*-pronunciation already insisted on in the sixteenth century.

ii, uu. Although long *ii* and *uu* were still preserved at the beginning of the Early Modern period, they soon began to be diphthongized. Salesbury writes *ei* and *ow*, as in *wein* (=*wiin*), *ddow* (=ðuu), probably meaning *éi, óu.* There seem also to be indications of a broader pronunciation, *əi, əu*, which, as we shall see, became general in the following period. It is, then, clear that *ii* and *uu* were first modified by partial lowering, *i-i, u-u*, becoming *é-i, ó-u*, and that the resulting diphthongs were then exaggerated by divergence—a not unfrequent phenomenon.

èè, éé, òò, óó. The history of these vowels in Modern English affords a striking example of the Teutonic tendency to narrow long vowels, each of them being raised a step, so that *éé* and *óó* become *ii* and *uu*, as in *diid*=Middle E. *déél* and *suun*=*sóón*, while *èè* and *òò* become *éé, óó*, as in *dréém*=Middle E. *drèèm* and *bóón*=*bòòn* (O.E. *bān*).

In one word, the Middle E. *òò* has been preserved up to the present day, and, we may therefore assume, in the Early Modern period also, namely, in the adj. *bròòd*=O.E. *brād.*

ai, au, eu, òòu, óóu. The Middle English diphthongs are generally preserved, although there are traces of the simplification of *ai* and *au*, which was fully carried out in the following period. *eu* was also simplified into *yy* in some words, such as *tryy, nyy*, while in others, such as *heu, sheu*, it was preserved. *óóu* did not, as might be expected, become *uu*, but its first element was kept unchanged, so that *blóóu* (=O.E. *blōwan*) has remained unchanged up to the present day. *òòu* seems to have changed regularly into *óóu, cnòòu* (=O.E. *cnāwan*) becoming *cnóóu*: the two *oous* were therefore levelled.

Quantity.

Middle English *èè* seems to have been shortened very early in the Modern period in some words which still preserve in writing the *ea*=Middle E. *èè*. Such words are *dèf, instèd, hèd, rèd* (partic.), *lèd* (subst.), *dèd, brèd*, and several others. Nearly all the cases, it will be observed, occur before *d*. We shall find the same tendency to shorten before a stopped consonant in the Late Modern period as well.

Consonant Influence.

The most important case is the development of *u* before *l* in the combinations *al* and *óól* (=Middle E. *òò*), *al, talk, óóld*, becoming *aul, taulk, óóuld*. The form *aul* is the origin of our present *òòl, tòòk*.

The only traces of *r*-influence, so marked in the present period, are shown in the occasional conversion of *e* into *a*, as in *hart, smart,* for the older *hert, smert.*

TRANSITION PERIOD.

We now come to the most important and difficult period of Modern English, in which the vowels of the language may be said to have broken away entirely from the Middle English traditions, and entered on a new life of their own. It is therefore fortunate that the phonetic authorities of this period are of a far higher stamp than those of the preceding one: many of their observations are extremely acute, and are evidently the result of careful study of the actions of the vocal organs.

SHORT VOWELS.

e, i, o, remain unchanged, as in the previous period. It is interesting to observe that we now, for the first time, find the qualitative distinction between short and long *i* and *u* recognized by one of Mr. Ellis's authorities. The following is Cooper's list of exact pairs of long and short vowel-sounds (E. E. P. p. 83).

1	2	3	4	5	6	7	8
can	ken	will	folly	full	up	meet	foot
cast	cane	weal	fall	foale	—	need	fool

which Mr. Ellis interprets thus (denoting the wide vowel by italics):

cæn	kèn	w*i*l	fòli	f*u*l	əp	mit	fut
cææst	kèèn	wéél	fòòl	fóól	—	niid	fuul

It is clear that, as Mr. Ellis remarks, Cooper was dissatisfied with the usual pairing of *i, ii,* and *u, uu* (*fil, fiil*), and therefore tried to find the true short-narrow *i* and *u* in *miit* and *fuut*, where the *ii* and *uu* were probably shortened before the voiceless *t*, as is still the case. Again, he lengthened the short wide *i* and *u*, and finding that the resulting long vowel was nearly identical with the mid-narrow *éé* and *óó*, naturally identified them as the true longs and shorts. It must be observed that the *u* of *fuut* has not only been shortened to *fut* in the present English, but has also had time to follow the usual tendencies of short vowels, and become wide. The shortening is, therefore, in all probability, of some antiquity. If, then, we suppose that the long *uu* of *fuut* had been shortened to *u* in Cooper's time, and had not yet been widened, we see that the pairing of *fut* and *fuul* may very well have been perfectly accurate, both as regards quality and quantity.

In the pairs *folly, fall,* Mr. Ellis makes the short *o* of *folly* to correspond exactly with the long *òò*, and assumes it to be narrow. This, I think, is unnecessary. It is clear that Cooper's analysis is not absolutely accurate; it is only a considerable step in advance. He may very well have considered the distinction between *òò* and *óó* quite minute enough, and may therefore have disregarded the further refinement of distinguishing narrow and wide *ò*.

a. The present *æ*-sound is clearly recognized by the seventeenth-century phoneticians. Wallis describes *a* (both long and short) as a palatal, as opposed to a guttural vowel —as being formed by compressing the air between the middle of the tongue and the palate with a wide opening. And the Frenchman Miege identifies the English short *æ* with the French *e ouvert*, which would certainly be the nearest equivalent.

u. The change of the old *u* into *ə* was fully established in the Transition period, and it is clear from the descriptions given of the sound that it closely resembled the present one: Wallis calls it an obscure sound, and compares it with the French *eu* in *serviteur*, while Miege compares it with the French *o*—a common error of foreigners at the present day, and both Wallis and Wilkins identify it with one of the pronunciations of Welsh *y*, which is generally identified with our *ə*.

Before going any further, it will be necessary to consider the present pronunciation, or rather pronunciations, of the *ə* more closely. There are two distinct sounds of the *ə*—the high-back-wide and the mid-back-narrow, which, although formed so differently, are so similar in sound that even a practised ear finds it often difficult to distinguish them. Besides these two, a third sound may be heard in many English and Scotch dialects, which is the low-back-narrow.

Different as these three vowels are, they all agree in being unrounded back vowels, and it is clear from the seventeenth century statements that the main distinction between *u* and *ə* was then, as it is now, that *u* was rounded, *ə* not. Now it is quite certain that *u* itself was, in the seventeenth century, the high-back-wide-round (which it still is in those words, such as *wulf*, in which the *u* has been exceptionally retained); unrounded, this vowel would naturally become the high-back-wide—the very sound still in common use. The probability that this was also the seventeenth-century sound is raised almost to a certainty by the statement of Wallis, that the sound is formed with the greatest of the three degrees of closeness of the lingual passage (between tongue and palate) recognized by him. Wilkins's statement that the sound is "framed by a free emission of the breath from the throat," and, again, that it is formed "without any particular motion of the tongue or lips," may be considered as evidence that some such sound as the present mid-back-narrow was also given to the *ə*, but it is quite as probable that the whole description is inaccurate.

The general conclusion I arrive at is, that *u* was first unrounded, and that the resulting high-back-wide was in some pronunciations imitated by the mid-back-narrow, which in some dialects was, in accordance with the tendencies of short vowels, brought down to the low position.

Long Vowels.

éé, óó. The close *éé* and *óó*=Middle English *èè* and *òò*, are distinctly recognized. Wallis states that "*e* profertur sono acuto claroque ut Gallorum *é* masculinum," and Cooper, as we have seen (p. 522), pairs *full* and *foal* as long and short, which he could not have done if the *oa* of *foal* still had the broad *òò*-sound.

éi, óu. The diphthongization of Middle English *ii* and *uu* is carried a step further than in the previous period; all the authorities agree in either identifying, or, at least, comparing the first element of the two diphthongs with the *ə* of *bət.* *wiin* and *ðuu* appear, therefore, in the Transition period as *wəin* and *ðəu*—very nearly their present form.

ai, au. An important change of this period, although partially developed, as Mr. Ellis has shown, much earlier, is the simplification of the old diphthongs *ai* and *au* into *ee-* and *oo*-vowels. Those writers of the Early period who acknowledge the simple sounds do not give any clue to their precise nature, but the seventeenth century accounts point clearly to *èè* and *òò*, which latter is the sound still preserved in such words as *lòò, hòòk=lau, hauk,* although *èè*, as in *dèè=dai,* has been moved up to *éé,* probably because the Early Modern *éé* has become *ii* in the present English.

The above changes were either already in operation in the Early Modern period, or were at least prepared by previous changes: the next two are peculiar to the Middle period.

aa. Long, like short, *aa* was changed to the front vowel *æ*, *naam* becoming *nææm.* The *ææ*, being a long vowel, was soon narrowed into *èè*, as is shown by Cooper's pairing *ken* (=*kèn*) and *cane* (=*kèèn*) as long and short.

yy. Long *yy*, both in English words such as *nyy*, and French such as *tyyn*, was diphthongized into *iu*, *nyy* and *tyyn* becoming *niu* and *tiun.* The older *yy* was, however, still preserved by some speakers, and we have the curious spectacle of the two contemporaries Wallis and Wilkins ignoring each other's pronunciations, Wilkins asserting that the sound of *yy* is "of laborious and difficult pronunciation," especially "to the English," while Wallis considered this very *yy*-sound to be the only English pronunciation of long *u*.

It was probably the influence of this new *iu* that changed the older *eu* into *iu, heu*, etc., becoming *hiu*, whence by consonantization of the first element of the diphthong the present *hyuu.*

IV.

HISTORICAL VIEW OF ENGLISH SOUND-CHANGES.

	Old English.	Middle English.	Modern English.
1	mann	man	mœn
	sæt (=sat)	sat	sæt
	heard (=hard)	hard	haəd
	nama	naam	néim
5	èndc (=andi)	ènd	ènd
	hélpan (=hilpan)	hèlp	hèlp
	seofon	seven	sevən
	mète (=mati)	mèèt	miit
	stélan (=stilan)	stèèl	stiil
10	sǣ (=saiw)	sèè	sii
	dǣd (=dūd)	déél	diid
	dreām (=draum)	drèèm	driim
	grēne	gréén	griin
	seō	séé	sii
15	witan	wit	wit
	hyll	hil	hil
	wīn	wiin	wain
	fȳr	fiir	fair
	óft (=ufta)	òft	òft
20	òn (=an)	òn	òn
	hól	hòòl	hóul
	tā	tòò	tóó
	tō	tóó	tuu
	sunu	sun	sʌn
25	hūs	huus	haus
	dæg	dai	déi
	sècgan	sei, sai	séi
	lagu	lau	lòò

LATE MODERN PERIOD.

The further changes of the eighteenth century are comparatively slight. The short vowels remain unchanged.

The only long vowels which undergo any modification are the *ees*. In the first place the *éés* of the preceding period are raised to *ii*, *dréém* becoming *driim*, the result being that the Middle English *èè* and *éé* are both confused under *ii*. The word *gréét*=M.E. *grèèt* (O.E. *greāt*) is an example of exceptional retention of the older *éé*.

èè from *aa* and *ai* is raised to the mid-position of *éé*, left vacant by the change of *ée* into *ii*, *nèèm* from *naam* and *sèè* from *sai* becoming *néém* and *séé*.

òò and *óó* are, on the other hand, retained unaltered. We see, therefore, that the fully-established pronunciation of the eighteenth century differed but slightly from that now in use.

Quantity.

The Early Modern *uu* from *óó* is often shortened before stops, almost always before *k*, frequently before other stops, and occasionally before other consonants. Examples are: *luk* (=Middle E. *lóók*), *tuk* (*tóók*), *buk* (*bóók*), *stud* (*stóód*), *gud* (*góód*), *fut* (*fóót*), *huf* (*hóóf*), *buzəm* (*bóózom*).

Other cases of shortening are doubtful, as they probably took place in the Early period: even the changes just considered may have been, at least partially, developed in the Transition period.

The lengthening of vowels before certain consonants will be considered in the next section.

Consonant Influence.

Some important modifications are produced in this period by consonant influence, which has, in some cases, also had a conservative effect in preserving older sounds, which would otherwise have undergone various modifications.

The most marked influence is that exercised by the *r*. So strong is it, indeed, that in the present English hardly any vowel has the same sound before *r* as before other consonants. One important result of this is that the *r* itself becomes a superfluous addition, which is not required for distinguishing one word from another, and is therefore weakened into a mere vocal murmur, or else dropped altogether, although always retained before a vowel.

The following table will give a general view of these modifications. The first column gives the Middle English vowels, the second gives what would be their regular representatives in Late Modern English, the third gives the forms they actually assume, and the last column gives examples with the Middle E. forms in parentheses:

ar	ær	aar	haaəd (hard)
ir	ir	əər	þəəd (þird)
èr	èr	əər	swəəv (swerv)
ur	ər	əər	təəf (turf)
òr	òr	òòr	nòòəþ (norþ)
aar	éér	èèr	fèèr (faar)
air	óér	èèr	fèèr (fair)
óér	iir	iiər (èèr)	diiər, ðèèr (dóór, ðóór)
èèr	iir	iiər (èèr)	iiər, bèèr (èèr, bèèr)
óór	uur	uuər, òòr	muuər, flòòr (móór, flóór)
òòr	óór	òòr	mòòr (mòòr)
iir	air	aiər	faiər (fiir)
uur	aur	auər	sauər (suur)

The sympathy between *r* and the broad (low or back) vowels, which is also shown in the older change of *ster*, etc., into *star*, is evident enough here also. In such words as *fèèr* the seventeenth-century sound of long *aa* has been preserved almost unchanged, while in *flòòr* the *r* has not only prevented the regular change into *uu*, but has even lowered the vowel from the *óó*- to the *òò*-position.

In many cases it is doubtful whether the influence of the *r* has been simply conservative, or whether the change—say of *hard* into *hærd*—actually took place, and that the influence of the *r* afterwards changed the *æ* into *a*. The change of *a* into *æ* certainly seems to have been fully carried out in the Transition period before *r* as well as the other consonants, if we may trust the phonetic authorities; but it is quite possible that the older *a*s may have remained throughout as vulgarisms, and soon have regained their lost ground.

The levelling of *ir*, *er*, and *ur*, which are kept quite distinct by the phoneticians of the Transition period, is a very curious phenomenon, as it has resulted in an entirely new vowel, which only occurs in these combinations. This vowel is the low-mixed-narrow. It is evidently closely allied to the regular short *ə* in *bət*, and it seems most probable that the first change was to level *ir*, *er*, and *ər* under *ər* (mid-back-narrow), which would then, by the further influence of the *r*, pass into the low-back-narrow, whence to the low-mixed-narrow is but a short step. Then the vowel was lengthened, and the *r* absorbed.

The influence of *l* is, like that of *r*, in the direction of broadening. In the combinations *alf* and *alm* original short *a* is preserved, the *l* is dropped and the vowel lengthened, so that *half* and *salm* (written *psalm*) become *haaf* and *saam*. In the Early period some of these words developed the usual *au*, but the present forms cannot have arisen from *au*, except, perhaps, *haam* from *halm*, which is often pronounced *hòòm*, pointing clearly to an older *haulm*.

Besides *r* and *l*, there are other consonants which tend to preserve the quality of short *a*, namely, ð, þ, *s* and *f*, although the *a* is generally lengthened: *faaðər*, *paaþ*, *graas*, *aask*, *laaf*, *craaft*. The refined Transition pronunciation *pæþ*, *æsk*, is, however, still to be heard.

Before leaving this subject of consonant influence, it is necessary to observe that the rules just stated do not always apply to dissyllables, but only to monosyllables. Thus we find *sælou*, *fælou*, not *sòlou*, *fòlou*, *nærou* not *narou*, and *gæðər* contrasting with *faaðər* and *raaðər*.

The influence of initial *w* is also very characteristic of Late Modern English. It not only preserves the old *u*, as in *wul*, *wulf*, but also regularly rounds short *a* into *ò*, *what*, *swan*, becoming *whòt*, *swòn*; also in dissyllables, such as *swòlóu*, *wòlóu*. The Transition forms *wəl*, *wəlf*, *whæt*, were probably artificial refinements, which were never accepted by the mass of the people.[1] (*See also* p. 151.)

LATEST MODERN PERIOD.

We are now, at last, able to study the sounds of our language, not through the hazy medium of vague descriptions and comparisons, but by direct observation; we can throw away theory, and trust to facts. If our analysis of speech-

[1] Mr. H. Nicol has just called my attention to the fact (which I had overlooked) that the change does not take place when the *a* is followed by a back consonant: *wæg*, *wæx*, etc.

sounds were perfectly accurate and exhaustive, and if our ears were trained to recognize with certainty every appreciable shade of pronunciation, the task would be easy enough. As it is, its difficulties are very great, and the observations I am about to make cannot therefore make any pretensions either to complete fullness or perfect accuracy. They are mere first attempts, and will require much revision.

Diphthongization.

The most prominent feature of our present English is its tendency to diphthongization.

The diphthongic character of our *éé* and *óó* has been distinctly recognized by our leading phoneticians, especially Smart and Bell.

Mr. Bell analyses the two diphthongs as *éi*, *óu*, but I find, as regards my own pronunciation, that the second elements are not fully developed *i* and *u*. In pronouncing *óu* the tongue remains throughout in the mid-position, and the second element only differs from the first in being formed with greater closure of the lips, so that it is an intermediate sound between *oo* and *uu*. In *éi* the tongue seems to be raised to a position half way between *é* and *i* in forming the second element, not to the full high position of *i*.

This indistinctness of the second elements of our *éi* and *óu* explains the difficulty many have in recognizing their diphthongic character. Mr. Ellis, in particular, insists strongly on the monophthongic character of his own *ee*s and *oo*s. I hear his *ee* and *oo* as distinct diphthongs, not only in his English pronunciation, but also in his pronunciation of French, German, and Latin.

The observation of existing pronunciations has further revealed a very curious and hitherto unsuspected fact, namely that our *ii* and *uu* are no longer pure monophthongs in the mouths of the vast majority of speakers, whether educated or uneducated. They are consonantal diphthongs, *ii* terminating in the consonant *y*, *uu* in *w*=*iy*, *uw*. The distinction between *bit* and *biit* (written *beat*) depends not on the short vowel being wide and the long narrow, but on the former being a monophthong, the latter a diphthong. The narrowness of *ii* (or rather *iy*) is therefore unessential, and we find, accordingly, that the first element of both *iy* and *uw* is generally made wide. These curious developments are probably the result of sympathetic imitation of *éi* and *óu;* and the tongue being already in the highest vowel position the only means of further contraction of the lingual passage left was the formation of consonants.

The only long vowels left are *aa* and *òò*. Are these genuine monophthongs? I believe not, although their diphthongic character is certainly not nearly so strongly marked as in the case of the vowels already considered. Nevertheless, these two vowels always seem to end in a slight vocal murmur, which might be expressed thus—*aaə, òòə*. I find that *aa* and *òò*, if prolonged ever so much, still have an abrupt unfinished character if this vocal murmur is omitted. The difference between *lòò* (written *law*) and *lòòə* (*lore*) is that in the former word the final *ə* is strictly diphthongic and half evanescent, while the *ə* of the second word is so clearly pronounced as almost to amount to a separate syllable. The distinction between the words written *father* and *farther* is purely imaginary.

In popular speech these diphthongs undergo many modifications. The first elements of *éi* and *óu* often follow the general tendencies of short vowels, and are lowered to the low-front-narrow and low-back-wide-round positions respectively, giving *èi* and *òu*. This peculiar exaggeration of the two diphthongs, which is not uncommon even among the educated, is popularly supposed to be a substitution of *ai* for *éi*, and those who employ it are reproached with saying "high" instead of "hay." I find, however, that those who say *hèi* for *héi* never confuse it with *hai*, which many of them pronounce very broadly, giving the *a* the low-back sound of the Scotch *man*.

The *ó* of *óu* is often, especially in affected pronunciation, moved forward to the mid-mixed-round position, and from there, by lowering and further shifting forwards, to the low-front-narrow-round position, so that *nóu* becomes *nœu*.

In like manner, the *u* of *uw*=*uu* is often weakened into the high-mixed-round (wide), which is nearly the German *ü*. So that *tuu* becomes almost *tyw* or *tüw*.

The two diphthongs corresponding to Middle E. *ii* and *uu* show strongly divergent tendencies in the present pronunciation. The first element of our *ai* is, I believe, the high-back-wide (which is also the commonest sound of the *ə* in *bət*), that of *au* the low-mixed-wide. In vulgar speech the distinction is still more marked, the *a* of *ai* being gradually lowered to the full low position, whilst the *a* of *au* is moved forward to the low-front-wide position, giving the familiar *æus* for *haus*. These exaggerations may be partly attributable to the desire to prevent confusion with the *èi* and *òu* arising from *éé* and *óó*.

The investigation of these peculiarities is not only of high scientific interest, but is also of great practical importance. We see that the imagined uniformity of "correct" pronunciation is entirely delusive—an error which only requires a little cultivation of the observing faculties to be completely dissipated.

It is also certain that the wretched way in which English people speak foreign languages—often in such a style as to be quite unintelligible to the natives—is mainly due to their persistently ignoring the phonetic peculiarities of their own language. When we once know that our supposed long vowels are all diphthongs, we are forced to acknowledge that the genuine *ii*s and *uu*s of foreign languages are really strange sounds, which require to be learnt with an effort, in the same way as we acquire French *u* or German *ch*. A case once came under my notice, in which the French word written *été* was confidently given forth as *èitèi*, on the strength of the grammar's assertion that the French *e aigu* had the sound of the English *ay* in *hay*. The result was, of course, to produce a word utterly unintelligible to a Frenchman.

Short Vowels.

The short vowels do not seem to have changed much in the last few generations. The most noticeable fact is the loss of *æ* among the vulgar. It is modified by raising the tongue into the mid-front-wide, resulting in the familiar *ceb* for *cæb*. This anomalous raising of a short vowel is gradually spreading among the upper classes, and is already quite fixed in many colloquial phrases, such as *nóu thenc yuw*, in which *thænc* is hardly ever pronounced with *æ*, as it should be theoretically. To keep the old original *e* distinct from this new sound, the original *e* generally has the broad sound of the low-front-narrow—a pronunciation which is very marked among the lower orders in London. In the pronunciation of those who retain *æ*, original *e* often has the thinner mid-front-wide sound.

Quantity.

The laws of quantity in the Latest Modern English, which are of a very peculiar and interesting character, were, as far as I know, never stated till I gave a brief account of them in the paper on Danish Pronunciation, already mentioned.

The distinction between long and short vowel is preserved strictly only in dissyllables. In monosyllables short vowels before single consonants are very generally lengthened, especially among the uneducated. If the vowel is kept short, the consonant must be lengthened. The result is, that short accented monosyllables do not exist in English. Either the vowel or the consonant must be long. If the vowel is naturally long, the consonant is shortened; if the vowel is originally short, the consonant is lengthened; or else the vowel is lengthened, and the consonant shortened. We thus obtain the forms *téil*, *tèll*, or *tèèl*, of which the last two are entirely optional. Although these quantitative distinctions are most clearly observable in the liquids, they apply quite as fully to the stops, as may be seen by any one who compares the English *hædd* and *hætt* with the Danish *hat*, in which the *t* is really short, giving a peculiarly abrupt effect to English ears.

Among the educated the form *tèll* is more frequent, but among the vulgar the lengthened *tèèl* is very common. These popular pronunciations are very interesting, as affording the only true undiphthongic long vowels which English now possesses: *fiil* and *fill* in popular speech are really *fiyl* and *fiil* with the same wide vowel, the only difference being that in the latter word it is perfectly homogeneous, while in the former it is consonantally diphthongized.

It also deserves notice that there are really three degrees of vowel quantity in English—short, medial, and long, the rule being that long vowels occur only before voice consonants or finally, while before breath consonants they become medial. Compare *luuz* with *luus*, *paaðz* with *paaþ*. This fact has been noticed by Dr. Murray, in his work on the Scotch Dialects (p. 98, note).

A similar distinction is observable in the quantity of some of the consonants themselves. Liquids and nasals are long before voice, short before breath consonants. Compare *billd* with *bilt*, *sinnz* with *sins*. This distinction of quantity has led Mr. Bell to assume that the *l* in *bilt* is voiceless, although he admits (Visible Speech, p. 67) that "there is a trace of vocality." That the *l* in the English *bilt* is *not* voiceless becomes at once evident on comparing it with the Icelandic *lt*, which is really *lht*, with a distinct hiss.

Consonant Influence.

Apart from the laws of quantity already discussed, there is little to say on this subject. There are, however, words whose present forms afford instructive examples of the influence of *l*. These words are *childrən* and *milk*, in both of which the *i* has been gutturalized and labialized into *u* by the *l*, which in the second word has further developed into the diphthong *yu*, giving *chuldrən* and *myulc*. The diphthong in *myulc* is somewhat puzzling. It is not impossible that the older forms were *chyyldrən* and *myylc*, which were then diphthongized into *yu*, which in the former word lost its *y*-consonant; or *chyldrən* may have developed direct into *chuldrən*. (*See note* *** on p. 163.)

NOTES ON THE CONSONANTS.[1]

H.

That initial *h* in Old English had the same sound as it has now, and not that of the German *ch* (*kh*), which it is generally agreed to have had when medial and final, is clear from its frequent omission, even in the older documents of the language; for if initial *h* had been really *kh*, there would be no more reason for its omission than for that of *s* or any other initial consonant.

During the Middle period the use of *h* to designate the sound of *kh* was abandoned in favour of *gh*, whence the present spellings *night*, *laugh*, for the O.E. *niht*, *hleahhan*. The spelling *ch*, as in German, also occurs, and it is, at first sight, difficult to see why it was not universally adopted instead of *gh*, which ought to express, not the breath sound *kh*, but rather the corresponding voice (as in German *sagen*). The simplest explanation seems to be that the *ch* was discarded in order to prevent confusion with the *ch* from *c* in *child*, *much*, etc.

HR, HL, HW, HN.

There can be no doubt that in the oldest pronunciation of these combinations the *h* was pronounced separately, and that at a still earlier period the *h* was a real *ch*. In Modern Icelandic, however, which is the only Teutonic language that still preserves all these sounds, the combinations have been simplified into *rh*, *lh*, *wh*, *nh*, which are nothing else but the breath sounds corresponding to *r*, *l*, *w*, *n*, respectively. Modern English also preserves one of them in the simplified form of *wh*.

[1] These do not lay claim to any fullness of detail: they are merely intended to serve as a stop-gap till it is possible to treat the subject more at length.

The fact that *hr*, *hl*, and *hn* drop their *h* very early in the Transition period, seems to show that the change from the compound *h-r*, etc., to the simplified *rh*, must have already begun in the Old English period. That they did pass through the stage of simplification is clear from the spellings *rh*, etc., as in *rhof* (Ormulum), *lhord* (Ayenbite), and the *wh* still preserved.

The change from *hl* to *l* is not, therefore, to be explained as the result of apocope of the initial *h*, but rather as a levelling of the voiceless *lh* under the voiced *l*—a change which is at the present moment being carried out with the only remaining sound of this group, the *wh*.

Þ, F.

The main difficulty here is to determine the laws which govern the distribution of the breath þ and *f*, and the voice ð and *v*. The following table gives a general view of the relations of the living languages.

English	... þing	... ðæt......	brəðər	óuþ
Icelandic	... þing	... þaað ...	brouðir	éið
Swedish	... ting	... det	bróódər	ééd
Danish	ting	... dé	bróóðər	ééð
Dutch	ding	... dat	brudər	ééd
German	... ding	... das	bruudər	aid (*for* ait)

The German *ait*, which is still written *eid*, really stands for *aid*, as final stops are always voiceless or whispered in German. The same is the case in Dutch, but original voiced stops preserve their vocality, if followed by a word beginning with a vowel.

The inferences suggested by this table are clear enough.

The English final þ for ð is evidently an exceptional change, which does not appear in any of the other languages. So also is the Icelandic þ in *þaað*. The majority, then, of the living Teutonic languages agree in showing ð medially and finally and þ initially, except in a small group of words in very common use, such as *the, then, thus, than, thou.*

The question now arises, what is the relation of the Dutch and German *d* in *ding* to the Scandinavian and English *ting, þing?* If the initial breath forms are the original ones, the voiced *ðat*, etc., must be later modifications; if the ð of *ðat* is the older, the *t* and þ of *ting* and *þing* must be the later developments—in short, there must have been a period in which þ did not exist at all.

If we go back to the Oldest English, we find no trace of any distinction between þ and ð. Many of the oldest MSS. write the ð in all cases—*ðing, ðæt, broðor, að*, while others write þ with equal exclusiveness. When we consider that ð is simply the usual *d* modified by a diacritic, and that the þ itself is, in all probability (as, I believe, was first suggested by Mr. Vigfússon), a D with the stem lengthened both ways, we are led to the unavoidable conclusion that the voice sound was the only one that existed in the Early Old English period. The fact that some of the very oldest remains of our language use the digraph *th* cannot outweigh the overwhelming evidence the other way. It was very natural to adopt the digraph *th*, which already existed in Latin as the representative of the sound *th*, as an approximate symbol of the voiced *dh*, but it is clear that it was considered an inaccurate representation of a voiced consonant, and was therefore abandoned in favour of þ or ð, which were at first employed indiscriminately.

Afterwards, when the breath sound developed itself, the two letters were utilized to express the difference, and þ, whose origin was of course forgotten, came to be regarded as the exclusive representative of the breath sound. Accordingly the later MSS. of the tenth and eleventh centuries always use both þ and ð *together*, often rather loosely, but always with the evident intention of writing þ initially, ð medially and finally. None of them seem to make any distinction between *þing* and *ðæt*, etc. It is, however, clear that these words must have had the same voice pronunciation as they have now.

We may therefore assume three stages in the history of the English *th*-sounds:

Early Old English ...	ðing......	ðæt......	brōðor......	āð
Late Old English ...	þing......	ðæt......	brōðor......	āð
Modern English	þing......	ðæt......	brəðər......	óuþ

The mystery of the pronunciation of *the, thou*, is now solved: these words are archaisms, preserved unchanged by the frequency of their occurrence.

These results apply equally to the *f*. There can be no doubt that the *f* in Early Old English was vocal like the Welsh *f*, as is shown by the Old German spelling *uolc*, etc. (still preserved, though the sound has been devocalized, in Modern German), and the Dutch pronunciation.

In the Transition period the voiced *f* was represented by the French *u*, as in Old German, and it is clear from such spellings as *vox* for *fox*, *uader* for *fader*, that the initial vocality of the Old English *f* (and consequently of the ð also) was still preserved, as it still is, in many of the Southern dialects.

Even in the present literary English we find initial vocality still preserved in the words *véin* (from *fana*), *væt* and *vixen*. As, however, these words are not of very frequent occurrence, it is not improbable that they were taken directly from one of the dialects.

There are a few cases of the retention of final vocality also, both of *f* and ð, in the present English. The words are *ov*, *twelv*, and *wið*, all three evidently preserved, like *ðæt*, etc., by their excessive frequency. The pronunciations *of* and *wiþ*, given by some of the Early Modern authorities, are made doubtful by their recognition of *ov* and *wið* as popular or vulgar pronunciations: they may therefore be purely artificial.

The vocal pronunciation of initial *s*, which is common in our dialects, and is shown for the fourteenth century by the Kentish *zay*, *zal*, etc., cannot be original. The sound of *z* is unknown in Scandinavia, and even in Germany the "soft" *s* is clearly the result of Low German influence, and it is unknown in the South German dialects.

It seems, therefore, that the vocalization of initial (and also medial) *s* in English is merely a case of levelling, caused by the analogy of the vocal ð and *v*.

G.

The use of *g* for the *y*-consonant (*j*) of the other languages is one of the knotty points of Old English phonetics. It is commonly assumed that the *g* of *gēr* (=Gothic *jēr*), *ge* (=*jus*), and the *ge* of *geoc* (=*juk*), *geā* (=*jā*), are merely orthographical expedients for indicating this *y*-consonant. But there seems no reason why the *i* of the other national orthographies should not have been adopted in England also. As a matter of fact, it is used in foreign names, as in *Iuþytte* (in the Chronicle), *Iuliana*, etc. And not only do such words as *geoc* alliterate with undoubted hard *g*s in the poetry, but we even find such pairs as *Juliana, god,* showing clearly that even in foreign words *y*-consonant was liable to be changed into a sound which, if not identical with the *g* of *god*, was at least very like it.

The *ge* of *geoc* makes it very probable that the *g*=*y*-consonant was a palatal sound—in short, a palatal stop formed in the place of *y* (=Sanskrit ज). The conversion of an open into a stopped consonant is, of course, anomalous, but precisely the same change has taken place in the Romance languages.

The spelling *cg* for *gg*, as in *liegan, ecg,* is curious. We can hardly suppose that the combination is to be understood literally as *c* followed by *g*. Such a change would, at least, be entirely without precedent, and it seems most probable that the combination was meant to indicate a whispered instead of a voiced *gg*. The peculiarity, whatever it was, does not seem to have been carried into the Middle period, whose scribes always write *gg*.

Final *g* after long vowels or consonants often becomes *h* in Old English, which, to judge from the spelling *bogh*=*bōh*=*bōg*, was originally vocal (=*gh*), although it was soon devocalized. In the Transition period all medial and final *g*s became open (*gh*), as in German, Danish, and Icelandic. This *gh* afterwards became palatalized after front, and labialized after back vowels (*ghw*), and in many cases the palatal and labial *gh* became still further weakened into *i* and *u*, forming the second elements of diphthongs. After a consonant the labial *gh* was confused with *w* (from which it differs only in being slightly more guttural), *folgian* becoming *folwen*. When the *w* came at the end of a word, it was weakened into *u*, *folw* becoming *folu*, and *malw* (O.E. *mealwe*) becoming *malu*. The present *óu* in *folóu*, for which there is sixteenth century authority, as well as for *folu*, is anomalous. It is possible that the *óu* pronunciation may be artificial—the result of the spelling *follow*.

Even initial *g* is often weakened before front vowels, so often, indeed, that the Old English form of the *g* (ȝ) came to be used exclusively to represent this weak sound, while the French form (nearly our present *g*) was reserved for the original stopped *g*. The first change was, no doubt into *gh*, *gifan* becoming *ghiven*, as in the Dutch *ghéévən*, which soon became palatalized, till at last it became simple *y*-consonant, as is clearly proved by such spellings as *iæf*=O.E. *geaf* (Peterborough Chronicle), *yelt*=*gylt* (Ayenbite), etc.

The *g* or *ge*, which represents original *y*-consonant in Old English, always undergoes this weakening, *geoc*, *gē*, becoming *yòòc*, *yéé*. Even when initial *ge* is merely the result of the diphthongization of *a* into *ea*, it is often weakened into *ya*, as in *yard*=*geard*=*gard*.

The result of all these changes was, that by the beginning of the sixteenth century *gh* was entirely lost, being either weakened into a vowel (*i* or *u*), or converted into the corresponding breath sound *kh*, but only finally, as in *dóóuh* (O.E. *dāg*), *enuuh* (*genōg*). In most cases final *gh* (when not vowelized) was dropped entirely, as in *fóóu* (*fāg*), *lóóu* (*lāg*), *fii* (*feoh*).[1]

In the present English *kh*—whether answering to O.E. *g* or *h*—has been entirely lost. It appears from Mr. Ellis's investigations that the full *kh* first became weakened to a

[1] The *u* in *dóóuh*, *fóóu(h)*, etc., was probably a mere secondary formation, generated by the *ghw*, the stages being *oogh*, *ooghw*, *ooughw*, and then *oouh* or simply *oou*.

mere aspiration, which was soon dropped. In such words as *niht* the *i* was lengthened, *niht* becoming *niit*, whence our present *nait*. Final *kh* preceded by a rounded vowel as in *lauh*, *enuuh*, was itself naturally rounded into *khw*, like the *kh* in the German *auch*; hence the present *laaf*, *enəf*—*laukh*, *lakhw*, *lawh*, *laf*. For fuller details the reader must be referred to Mr. Ellis's great work.

CH, J

The change of *c* into *ch* before and after front vowels, as in *chiild*, *tèèch*, from *cild*, *tǣcan*, offers considerable difficulties, on account of the many intermediate stages there must have been between the back stop *c* and the present *tsh*-sound. There can be no doubt that the first change was to move *c* to the front-stop position, but, although the further change to the point formation is simple enough, it is not easy to explain the intrusion of the *sh*: we would expect *ciild* to change simply into *tiild*, just as *gemaca* becomes *maat*. I believe that the change from the intermediate front-stop to *tsh* is a purely imitative one. If the front-stop is pronounced forcibly—even with a degree of force stopping far short of actual aspiration—the escape of breath after the contact is removed naturally generates a slight hiss of *yh* (as in *hue*), which is very like *sh* in sound—hence the substitution of the easier *tsh*.

The same remarks apply also to the *dzh*-sound in *wej*, *ej*, *rij*, etc., from *wecg*, *ecg*, *hrycg*.

It is instructive to observe the analogous changes in the Scandinavian languages. In Icelandic *k* and *g* before front vowels are shifted forward a little, without, however, losing their back character, almost as in the old-fashioned London pronunciation of *kaind*, *skai*, etc. In Swedish *k* before front vowels has a sound which is generally identified with the English *ch*. If, however, my limited observations are correct, the real sound is the front stop followed by the corresponding open breath (*yh*). The sound is certainly not the English *ch*, which the Swedes consider an unfamiliar sound. In

Norwegian the stopped element is dropped entirely, and nothing remains but a forward *yh*, so that *kenna* is pronounced *yhenna*. Both in Norwegian and Swedish *g* before front vowels has the simple sound of the consonant *y*.

SH.

The change of Old English *sc* into *sh* is not exactly parallel with that of *c* into *ch*, as it takes place after back as well as front vowels—not only in such words as *ship* (=*scip*), but also in *shun* (*āscunian*), etc. It is therefore possible that *sc* may have passed through the stage of *skh*, as in Dutch, a change which seems to be the result of the influence of the *s*, the *kh* instead of *k* being, like *s*, a sibilant unstopped consonant. The Old English spellings *sceacan*, *sceoc*, etc., for *scacan*, *scōc*, however, seem to point rather to a palatalization of the *c* at an early period. Whatever the development may have been, it is certain that the sound soon became simple, for we find it often written *ss* in the Early Middle period.

In Swedish the sound of *sh* is fully developed, but only before front vowels. In Norwegian *sk* before front vowels changes its *k* into *yh* (voiceless *y*-consonant), which, as we have already seen, is the regular change, giving the combination *s-yh*, which is generally confounded with simple *sh* by foreigners. These facts tend strongly to confirm the view that the change of *sk* into *sh* in English also is due to palatalization of the *k*, although we cannot determine with certainty what the intermediate stages were.

WORD LISTS.

The following lists are intended to include the majority of the words of Teutonic—that is to say English or Scandinavian—origin still in common use, with the corresponding Old and Middle forms. The first column gives the Old English forms; the second the Middle English (but without the final *e*, p. 56) as deduced from the Old English forms and the present traditional spelling, which is given in the third column; the fourth, lastly, gives the present sounds. I have, of course, carefully compared the valuable pronouncing vocabulary of Early Modern English given by Mr. Ellis in his Third Part, especially in all cases of irregular change or anomalous spelling. These exceptions will be considered hereafter.

The words are arranged primarily according to their vowels in the following order:—a (æ, ea, ei), ā, i, ī, ỵ, ȳ, é (eo), è, ē, ǣ=éé, ǣ=èè, eā, eō, u, ū, o, ō. Then according to the consonant that follows the vowel in this order: h, r, l, ð, s, w, f, ng, n, m, g, c, d, t, b, p; and lastly according to the initial consonant in the same order. The principle I have followed is to begin with the vowels, as being the most independent elements of speech, and to put the stops at the extreme end as being most opposed to the vowels. The semivowels or open consonants naturally come after the vowels, and the nasals next to the stops. As regards position, back consonants come first, then front, then point, and then lip. Voice consonants, of course, come before breath. It will easily be seen that the same general principles have been followed in the arrangement of the vowels. The order of position is back, mixed, front; high comes before mid, and mid before low, and round last of all.

To facilitate reference, I have often given the same word under as many different heads as possible, especially in cases of irregular development.

Old English forms which do not actually occur, but are postulated by later ones, are marked with an asterisk.

The Middle English forms in parentheses are those which, although not deducible from the spelling, are supported by other evidence.

Norse words are denoted by N., and the conventional Icelandic spellings are occasionally added in parentheses.

Many of the inorganic preterites (such as *bore*=*bær*) have been included in the present lists: they are all marked with a dagger.

a, æ, ea, ò.

OLD.	MIDDLE.		MODERN.	
hleahhan	lauh		*laugh*	laaf
geseah	sau		*saw*	sòò
eahta	eiht (ai)		*eight*	éit
hleahtor	lauhter	4	*laughter*	laaftər
sleaht	slauhter		*slaughter*	slòòtər
feaht	fauht		*fought*	fòòt
tǣhte	tauht		*taught*	tòòt
aron	ar	8	*are*	aar
hara	haar		*hare*	hèər
scearu	shaar		*share*	shèər
starian	staar		*stare*	stèər
sparian	spaar	12	*spare*	spèər
wær	waar		*ware (wary)*	wèər
faran	faar		*fare*	fèər
nearu (nearw-)	naru		*narrow*	nærou
caru	caar	16	*care*	cèər
dear	daar		*dare*	dèər
tær	† tòòr		*tore*	tòər
bær (*adj.*)	baar		*bare*	bèər
bær (*pret.*)	baar	20	*bare*	bèər
	† bòòr		*bore*	bòər
ears	ars		*arse*	aəs
ar(e)we	aru		*arrow*	æróu
spearwa	sparu	24	*sparrow*	spæróu
gearwa	gèèr		*gear*	giər
hærfest	harvest		*harvest*	haəvest
(ge)earnian	èèrn		*earn*	əən
wearnian	warn	28	*warn*	wòən
fearn	fern		*fern*	fəən
gearn	yarn		*yarn*	yaən
earm	arm		*arm*	aəm
hearm	harm	32	*harm*	haəm
wearm	warm		*warm*	wòəm
swearm	swarm		*swarm*	swòəm
earc	arc		*ark*	aəc
ærce-	arch-	36	*arch(bishop)*	aəch-

a(æ ea ei), i, é(eo), è, ē, ǣ, eā, eō, u, o.

a, æ, ea, ò (*continued*).

OLD.	MIDDLE.		MODERN.	
lāwerce	larc		*lark*	laəc
stearc	starc		*stark*	staəc
spearca	sparc		*spark*	spaəc
mearc	marc	40	*mark*	maəc
barc, N. (börkr)	barc		*bark*	baəc
pearruc	parc		*park*	paəc
heard	hard		*hard*	haəd
weard	ward	44	*ward*	wòəd
geard	yard		*yard*	yaəd
beard	bèèrd		*beard*	biəd
(ðū) eart	art		*art*	aət
sweart	swart	48	*swarthy*	swòəþi
cræt	cart		*cart*	caət
teart	tart		*tart*	taət
hearpe	harp		*harp*	haəp
scearp	sharp	52	*sharp*	shaəp
alor (*under* ld)				
ealu	aal		*ale*	éil
eall	al		*all*	òòl
heall	hal		*hall*	hòòl
salu (sealw-)	salu	56	*sallow*	sælou
smæl	smal		*small*	smòòl
sceal	shal		*shall*	shæl
scealu	scaal, shaal		*scale, shale*	scéil, shéil
steall	stal	60	*stall*	stòòl
weall	wal		*wall*	wòòl
hwæl	whaal		*whale*	whéil
falu (fealw-)	falu		*fallow*	fælóu
feallan	fal	64	*fall*	fòòl
nihtegale	nihtingaal		*nightingale*	naitinggéil
gealle	gal		*gall*	gòòl
calu (cealw-)	calu		*callow*	cælóu
ceallian (N. ?)	cal	68	*call*	còòl
dæl	daal		*dale*	déil
talu	taal		*tale*	téil
bealu	baal		*bale*	béil
swealwe	swalu	72	*swallow*	swolóu
wealwian	walu		*wallow*	wolóu
mealwe	malu		*mallow*	mælóu

h; r, hr, l, hl; ð, s, w, hw, f; ng, n, m; g, c, d, t, b, p.

a, æ, ea, ò (*continued*).

OLD	MIDDLE.		MODERN.	
ælf	elf		*elf*	elf
healf	half	76	*half*	haaf
sealfian	salv		*salve*	sælv
cealf	calf		*calf*	caaf
ælmesse	alms		*alms*	aamz
healm	halm	80	*halm*	hòòm
sealm	salm		*psalm*	saam
hālgian	halu		*hallow*	hælóu
gealga	galuz		*gallows*	gælóuz
tælg	talu	84	*tallow*	tælóu
stealcian	stalc		*stalk*	stòòc
wealcan	walc		*walk*	wòòc
bealca	balc		*balk*	bòòc
bealcettan	belch	88	*belch*	belch
alor	alder		*alder*	òòldər
eald	òòld		*old*	óuld
ealdormann	alderman		*alderman*	òòldəmən
healdan	hòòld	92	*hold*	hóuld
sealde	sòòld		*sold*	sóuld
fealdan	fòòld		*fold*	fóuld
ceald	còòld		*cold*	cóuld
tealde	tòòld	96	*told*	tóuld
beald	bòòld		*bold*	bóuld
healt	halt		*halt*	holt
sealt	salt		*salt*	solt
mealt	malt	100	*malt*	molt
hæ(f)ð	haþ		*hath*	hæþ
hraðor	raðer		*rather*	raaðər
hwæðer	wheðer		*whether*	wheðər
bæð	baþ	104	*bath*	baaþ
baðian	baað		*bathe*	béið
pæð	paþ		*path*	paaþ
fæðm	faðom		*fathom*	fæðəm
ea(l)swā	az	108	*as*	æz
assa	as		*ass*	aas
*hæ(f)s	haz		*has*	hæz

a(æ ea ei), i, é(eo), è, ē, ǣ, eā, eō, u, o

a, æ, ea, o (*continued*).

OLD.	MIDDLE.		MODERN.	
læssa	les		*less*	les
ðȳ læs ðe	lest	112	*lest*	lest
wæs	waz		*was*	woz
næs	nes		*ness*	nes
græs	gras		*grass*	graas
glæs	glas	116	*glass*	glaas
bræs	bras		*brass*	braas
æsc	ash		*ash*	æsh
āscian	asc		*ask*	aasc
ascan	ashez	120	*ashes*	æshez
rasc N.	rash		*rash*	ræsh
wascan	wash		*wash*	wosh
flasce	flasc		*flask*	flaasc
baða sic N.	basc	124	*bask*	baasc
la(to)st	last		*last*	laast
læst (*superl.*)	lèèst		*least*	liist
lǣstan	last		*last*	laast
fæst	fast	128	*fast*	faast
mæst	mast		*mast*	maast
gæst	gest		*guest*	gest
casta N.	cast		*cast*	caast
castel	castl	132	*castle*	caasl
blǣst	blast		*blast*	blaast
æsp	aspen		*aspen*	æspen
awel	aul		*awl*	òòl
clawu	clau	136	*claw*	clòò
hafa (*imper.*)	hav		*have*	hæv
behafa	behaav		*behave*	behéiv
hæfen	haaven		*haven*	héivon
hafoc	hauc	140	*hawk*	hòòc
stæf	staf		*staff*	staaf
stafas	staavz		*staves*	stéivz
sċafan	shaav		*shave*	shéiv
nafu	naav	144	*nave*	néiv
geaf	gaav		*gave*	géiv
græf } grafan }	graav		*grave*	gréiv
ceaf	chaf		*chaff*	chaaf
ceafor	chaafer	148	*(cock)chafer*	chéifər

h; r, hr, l, hl; ð, s, w, hw, f; ng, n, m; g, c, d, t, b, p.

a, æ, ea, o (*continued*).

OLD.	MIDDLE.		MODERN.	
crafian	craav		*crave*	créiv
clæfer	clòòver		*clover*	clóuvər
hæfð (*under* ð)				
hræfn	raaven		*raven*	réivən
hæfde } (*under* d)				
hlǣfdige }				
æfter	after	152	*after*	aaftər
sceaft	shaft		*shaft*	shaaft
cræft	craft		*craft*	craaft
angel (*hook*)	angl		*to angle*	ængl
hangan	hang	156	*hang*	hæng
hrang	rang		*rang*	ræng
lang	long		*long*	long
þrang	þrong		*throng*	þrong
þwang	þong	160	*thong*	þong
sang (*pret.*)	sang		*sang*	sæng
sang (*subst.*)	song		*song*	song
strang	strong		*strong*	strong
sprang	sprang	164	*sprang*	spræng
wrang (*pret.*)	wrang		*wrang*	ræng
wrang (*adj.*)	wrong		*wrong*	rong
fang	fang	167	*fang*	fæng
mangere	? monger (u)		*monger*	məngər
òn gemang	? among (u).		*among*	əməng
gang	gang		*gang*	gæng
tange	tongs		*tongs*	tongz
banga N	bang	172	*bang*	bæng
ancleow	ancl		*ankle*	æncl
ranc	ranc		*rank*	rænc
hlanc	lanc		*lank*	lænc
þancian	þanc	176	*thank*	þænc
sanc	sanc		*sank*	sænc
scranc	shranc		*shrank*	shrænc
stanc	stanc		*stank*	stænc
dranc	dranc	180	*drank*	drænc
ǣnig	aani (a)		*any*	eni
hanep	hemp		*hemp*	hemp

a(æ ea ei), i, é(eo), è, ē, ǣ, eā, eō, u, o.

a, æ, ea, ò (*continued*).

OLD.	MIDDLE.		MODERN.	
rann	ran		*ran*	ræn
rannsaca N.	ransac	184	*ransack*	rænsæc
lane	laan		*lane*	léin
ðanne {	ðan		*than*	ðæn
	ðen		*then*	ðen
swan	swan	188	*swan*	swon
gespann	span		*span*	spæn
wann (*pret.*)	† wun		*won*	won
wann (*adj.*)	wan		*wan*	won
wanian	waan	192	*wane*	wéin
hwanne	when		*when*	when
fana	vaan		*vane*	véin
mann	man		*man*	mæn
mane	maan	196	*mane*	méin
manig	maani (a)		*many*	meni
begann	began		*began*	begæn
ganot	ganet		*ganet*	gænet
cann	can	200	*can*	cæn
crana	craan		*crane*	créin
bana	baan		*bane*	béin
gebann	ban		*ban*	bæn
panne	pan	204	*pan*	pæn
an(d)swarian	answer		*answer*	aansər
anfilt	anvil		*anvil*	ænvil
and	and		*and*	ænd
hand	hand	208	*hand*	hænd
land	land		*land*	lænd
sand	sand		*sand*	sænd
standan	stand		*stand*	stænd
strand	strand	212	*strand*	strænd
wand N. (vöndr)	wand		*wand*	wond
wand (*pret.*)	† wuund		*wound*	waund
wandrian	wander		*wander*	wondər
candel	candl	216	*candle*	cændl
band (*pret.*)	† buund		*bound*	baund
band (*subst.*) {	band		*band*	bænd
	bond		*bond*	bond
brand	brand	220	*brand*	brænd
wanta, N.	want		*want*	wont
plantian	plant		*plant*	plaant

h; r, hr, l, hl; ð, s, w, hw, f; ng, n, m; g, c, d, t, b, p.

a, æ, ea, ò (*continued*).

OLD	MIDDLE.		MODERN.	
ic eam	am		*am*	æm
ǣmette	emet	224	*emmet, ant*	emet, aant
hamor	hamer		*hammer*	hæmər
ramm	ram		*ram*	ræm
lama (*adj.*)	laam		*lame*	léim
same	saam	228	*same*	séim
swamm	swam		*swam*	swæm
scamu	shaam		*shame*	shéim
fram	from		*from*	from
nama	naam	232	*name*	néim
gamen	gaam		*game*	géim
crammian	cram		*cram*	cræm
cwam	caam		*came*	céim
damm	dam	236	*dam*	dæm
tama (*adj.*)	taam		*tame*	téim
lamb	lamb		*lamb*	læm
wamb	wóómb		*womb*	wuum
camb	còòmb	240	*comb*	cóum
damp (*subst.*) N.	damp		*damp* (adj.)	dæmp
haga	hau		*haw*	hòò
læg	lai		*lay*	léi
lagu	lau	244	*law*	lòò
sage } sagu }	sau		*saw*	sòò
slagan	slai		*slay*	sléi
wagian	wag		*wag*	wæg
fleagan	flai	248	*flay*	fléi
mæg	mai		*may*	méi
maga	mau		*maw*	mòò
gnagan	gnau		*gnaw*	nòò
dæg	dai	252	*day*	déi
*dagenian	daun		*dawn*	dòòn
dragan {	drag		*drag*	dræg
	drau		*draw*	dròò
fæg(e)r	fair	256	*fair*	fèər
hæg(e)l	hail		*hail*	héil
snæg(e)l	snail		*snail*	snéil
næg(e)l	nail		*nail*	néil
tæg(e)l	tail	260	*tail*	téil

a, æ, ea, ȯ (*continued*).

OLD.	MIDDLE.		MODERN.	
æg𝑑er	ei𝑑er		*either*	ii𝑑ər ai𝑑ə
slæg(e)n	slain		*slain*	sléin
fæg(e)n	fain		*fain*	féin
mæg(e)n	main	264	*main*	méin
ongæg(e)n	again		*again*	əgéin əgèn
bræg(e)n	brain		*brain*	bréin
sægde	said		*said*	sed
mægd	maid	268	*maid*	méid
æcer	aacr		*acre*	éicər
æcern	aacorn		*acorn*	éicòən
race	raac		*rake*	réic
þæc	þach	272	*thatch*	þæch
rannsaca N.	ransac		*ransack*	rænsæc
sacu	saac		*sake*	séic
snaca	snaac		*snake*	snéic
scacan	shaac	276	*shake*	shéic
stacu	staac		*stake*	stéic
spræc	spaac †spòòc		*spake* *spoke*	spéic spóuc
wacan	waac	280	*wake*	wéic
wræc	wrec		*wreck*	rec
nacod	naaced		*naked*	néiced
macian	maac		*make*	méic
caca N.	caac	284	*cake*	céic
cwacian	cwaac		*cwake*	cwéic
taca N.	taac		*take*	téic
bæc	bac		*back*	bæc
bacan	baac	288	*bake*	béic
bræc	braac †bròòc		*brake* *broke*	bréic bróuc
blæc	blac		*black*	blæc
eax	ax	292	*axe*	æx
axan āxian (*under* sc)				
weax weaxan	wax		*wax*	wæx
fleax	flax		*flax*	flæx

h; r, hr, l, hl; 𝑑, s, w, hw, f; ng, n, m; g, c, d, t, b, p.

a, æ, ea, ò (*continued*).

OLD.	MIDDLE.		MODERN.	
ædesc	adis		*addice, adze*	ædz
hæ(f)de	had	296	*had*	hæd
hladan {	laad		*lade*	léid
	lòòd		*load*	lóud
hlæder	lader		*ladder*	lædər
hlǣ(f)dige	laadi	300	*lady*	léidi
sæd	sad		*sad*	sæd
sadol	sadl		*saddle*	sædl
sceadu	shadu		*shadow, shade*	shædóu, shéid
wadan	waad	304	*wade*	wéid
fæder	faðer		*father*	faaðər
gema(c)od	maad		*made*	méid
gegadorian	gaðer		*gather*	gæðər
tōgædere	togeðer	308	*together*	tugeðər
glæd	glad		*glad*	glæd
cradol	craadl		*cradle*	créidl
*geclǣðed	clad		*clad*	clæd
træd	†trod	312	*trod*	†trod
nædre	ader		*adder*	ædər
blæd	blaad		*blade*	bléid
blædre	blader		*bladder*	blædər

æt *(prep.)*	at	316	*at*	æt
æt *(pret.)*	aat		*ate*	éit, et
hatian	haat		*hate*	héit
hætt	hat		*hat*	hæt
læt (lata)	laat	320	*late*	léit
þæt	ðat		*that*	ðæt
sæt	sat		*sat*	sæt
sæterdæg	saturdai		*saturday*	sætədi
wæter	water	324	*water*	wòòtər
hwæt	what		*what*	whot
spǣtte *(pret.)*	spat		*spat*	spæt
fæt	vat		*vat*	væt
fǣtt *(adj.)*	fat	328	*fat*	fæt
flat N.	flat		*flat*	flæt
geat *(subst.)*	gaat		*gate*	géit
begeat *(pret.)*	got		*got*	got
gnætt	gnat	332	*gnat*	næt
catt	cat		*cat*	cæt

crabba	crab		*crab*	cræb

a(æ ea ei), i, é(eo), è, ē, ǣ, eā, eō, u, o.

a, æ, ea, ǫ (*continued*).

OLD.	MIDDLE.		MODERN.	
apa	aap		*ape*	éip
happ N.	hapi	336	*happy*	hæpi
scapan	shaap		*shape*	shéip
æppel	apl		*apple*	æpl
sæp	sap		*sap*	sæp
hnæppian	nap	340	*nap*	næp
gẹapian	gaap		*gape*	géip
cnapa	cnaav		*knave*	néiv
papol(stān)	pebl		*pebble*	pebl

ei (ey). (*All Norse.*)

ei	ai	344	*aye*	ai, éi
þei(r) N.	ðai (ei)		*they*	ðéi
nei	nai		*nay*	néi
þeirra N.	ðeir		*their*	ðèər
heil	hail	348	*hail!*	héil
reisa	raiz		*raise*	réiz
hrein N.	rain(déér)		*rein(deer)*	réin(diər)
swein	swain		*swain*	swéin
steic	stèèc	352	*steak*	stéic
weic	wèèc		*weak*	wiic
beita	bait		*bait*	béit
deyja	dii		*die*	dai

ā.

rā	ròò	356	*roe*	róu
lā	lòò		*lo!*	lóu, lòò
slā	slòò		*sloe*	slóu
swā	sòò		*so*	sóu
wā	wòò	360	*woe*	wóu
hwā	hwóó		*who*	huu

h; r, hr, l, hl; ð, s, w, hw, f; ng, n, m; g, c, d, t, b, p.

ā (*continued*).

OLD.	MIDDLE.		MODERN.	
frā N.	fròò		*(to and) fro*	fróu
nā	nòò		*no*	nóu
(ic) gā	gòò	364	*go*	góu
dā	dòò		*doe*	dóu
tā	tòò		*toe*	tóu
twâ	twóó		*two*	tuu
āhte	òòuht	368	*ought*	òòt
(n)āht	(n)auht		*(n)aught*	(n)òòt
	not		*not*	not
hāl	hòòl / hwòòl		*whole*	hóul
	haal	372	*hale*	heil
hālgian (*under* a)				
māl	mòòl		*mole*	móul
gedāl	dòòl		*dole*	dóul
ār	òòr		*oar*	òər
hār	hòòr	376	*hoar*	hòər
rārian	ròòr		*roar*	ròər
lār	lòòr		*lore*	lòər
sār	sòòr		*sore*	sòər
māre	mòòr	380	*more*	mòər
gāre	gòòr		*gore*	gòər
geāra	yòòr		*yore*	yòər
bār	bòòr		*boar*	bòər
hlā(f)ord	lord	384	*lord*	lòəd
āð	òòþ		*oath*	óuþ
wrāð	wraþ		*wrath*	raaþ
	wròòþ		*wroth*	rò(ò)þ
lāðian	lòòð	388	*loathe*	lóuð
nā(n)þing	noþing		*nothing*	nəþing
clāð	cloþ		*cloth*	clò(ò)þ
clāðian	clòòð		*clothe*	clóuð
bāðir, N.	bòòþ	392	*both*	bóuþ
hās	hòòrs		*hoarse*	hòòəs
ārās	aròòz		*arose*	əróuz
þās	ðòòz		*those*	ðóuz
*hwās	whòòz	396	*whose*	huuz

ā (*continued*).

OLD.	MIDDLE.		MODERN.	
āscian (*under* a)				
*māst	mòòst		*most*	móust
gāst	gòòst		*ghost*	góust
lāwerce (*under* a)				
þāwan	þau	400	*thaw*	þòò
þrāwan	þròòu		*throw*	þró
sāwan	sòòu		*sow*	sóu
snāw	snòòu		*snow*	snóu
māwan	mòòu	404	*mow*	móu
crāwan	cròòu		*crow*	cróu
cnāwan	cnòòu		*know*	nóu
blāwan	blòòu		*blow*	blóu
sāwl	sòòul	408	*soul*	sóul
āwðer (=āhwæðer)	or		*or*	òɔr
gesāw(e)n	sòòun		*sown*	sóun
geþrāw(e)n	þròòun		*thrown*	þróun
gecnāw(e)n	cnòòun	412	*known*	nóun
hlāf	lòòf		*loaf*	lóuf
hlāford (*under* r)				
drāf	dròòv		*drove*	dróuv
ān	òòn, an, a		*one, an, a*	wɔn, ɔn, ə
ānlice	òònli	416	*only*	óunli
lān N.	lòòn		*loan*	lóun
nān	nòòn		*none*	nɔn
scān	shòòn		*shone*	shon
stān	stòòn	420	*stone*	stóun
? mānian	mòòn		*moan*	móun
gegān (*part.*)	gòòn		*gone*	gon
grānian	gròòn		*groan*	gróun
bān	bòòn	424	*bone*	bóun
hām	hòòm		*home*	hóum
lām	lòòm		*loam*	lóum
hwām	whóóm		*whom*	huum
fām	fòòm	428	*foam*	fóum
clām	clami		*clammy*	clæmi

h; r, hr, l, hl; ð, s, w, hw, f; ng, n, m; g, c, d, t, b, p.

ā (*continued*).

OLD.	MIDDLE.		MODERN.	
āgan	òòu		*owe*	óu
lāg	lòòu		*low*	lóu
fāg	fòò	432	*foe*	fóu
dāg	dòòuh		*dough*	dóu
āg(e)n	òòun		*own*	óun
āc	òòc		*oak*	óuc
(wed)lāc	(wed)loc	436	(*wed*)*lock*	(wed)loc
strācian	stròòc		*stroke*	stróuc
spāca	spòòc		*spoke*	spóuc
tācen	tòòcen		*token*	tóucən
-hād	-hóód	440	(*man*)*hood*	-hud
rād	ròòd		*rode, road*	róud
lād	lòòd(stòòn)		*load*(*stone*)	lóud(stóun)
wād	wòòd		*woad*	wóud
gād	gòòd	444	*goad*	góud
tāde	tòòd		*toad*	tóud
ābād	abòòd		*abode*	əbóud
brād	bròòd		*broad*	bròòd
? ādl				
āte	òòts	448	*oats*	óuts
hāt	hot		*hot*	hot
swāt (*under* ǣ = èè)				
wāt	wot		*wot*	wot
wrāt	wròòt		*wrote*	róut
gāt	gòòt	452	*goat*	góut
bāt	bòòt		*boat*	bóut
rāp	ròòp		*rope*	róup
sāpe	sòòp		*soap*	sóup
swāpan (*under* ǣ = éé)				
grāpian	gròòp	456	*grope*	gróup
pāpa	pòòp		*pope*	póup

ī.

riht	riht	*right*	rait
gelīhtan	liht	(*a*)*light*	lait

i (*continued*).

OLD.	MIDDLE.		MODERN.	
gesihð	siht	460	*sight*	sait
wiht	wiht		*wight*	wait
	whit		*whit*	whit
niht	niht		*night*	nait
miht	miht	464	*might*	mait
cniht	cniht		*knight*	nait
briht	briht		*bright*	brait
pliht	pliht		*plight*	plait
hire	hir (e)	468	*her*	həər
scire	shiir		*shire*	shiiər, shaiər
stīgrāp	stirup		*stirrup*	stirəp
cirice (*under* y)				
mirhð	mirþ		*mirth*	məəþ
wirsa (*under* y)				
hirde	herd	472	*(shep)herd*	(shep)əd
*þirda (=þridda)	þird		*third*	þəəd
*bird(=bridd)	bird		*bird*	bəəd
ill N.	il		*ill*	il
scilling	shiling	476	*shilling*	shiling
scil N.	scil		*skill*	scil
stille	stil		*still*	stil
spillan	spil		*spill*	spil
willa	wil	480	*will*	wil
wilig	wilu		*willow*	wilóu
gillan	yel		*yell*	yel
til N. (*prep.*) / tilian	til		*till*	til
bill	bil	484	*bill*	bil
film(en)	film		*film*	film
seoloc	silc		*silk*	silc
swilc (*under* c)				
hwilc (*under* c)				
meolc	milc		*milk*	milc
scild	shiild	488	*shield*	shiild
wilde	wiild		*wild*	waild
milde	miild		*mild*	maild

h; r, hr, l, hl; ð, s, w, hw, f; ng, n, m; g, c, d, t, b, p.

i (*continued*).

OLD	MIDDLE		MODERN	
gild	gild		*guild*	gild
gildan	yiild	492	*yield*	yiild
cild	chiild		*child*	chaild
cildru	children		*children*	children
hilt	hilt		*hilt*	hilt
smið	smiþ	496	*smith*	smiþ
wið	wið		*with*	wið
fiðele	fidl		*fiddle*	fidl
niðer	neðer		*nether*	neðəɹ
piða	piþ	500	*pith*	piþ
is	iz		*is*	iz
his	hiz		*his*	hiz
þis	ðis		*this*	ðis
*þise	ðèèz	504	*these*	ðiiz
mis-	mis-		*mis(take)*	mis-
missan	mis		*miss*	mis
gise	yis (e)		*yes*	yes
bliss	blis	508	*bliss*	blis
fisc	fish		*fish*	fish
disc	dish		*dish*	dish
biscop	bishop		*bishop*	bishəp
wīsdōm	wizdom	512	*wisdom*	wizdəm
list	list		*list*	list
þistel	þistl		*thistle*	þisl
mist	mist		*mist*	mist
gist	yèèst	516	*yeast*	yiist
misteltā	mistltòò		*mistletoe*	misltóu
Crist	Criist		*Christ*	Craist
cristenian	cristen		*christen*	crisn
gist	yèèst	520	*yeast*	yiist
gistrandæg	yisterdai (e)		*yesterday*	yestədi
hwistlian	whistl		*whistle*	whisl
wlisp (*adj.*)	lisp		*to lisp*	lisp
hwisprian	whisper	524	*whisper*	whispər
siwian	seu		*sew*	sóu
niwe	neu		*new*	nyuu

a(æ ea ei), i, ĕ(eo), è, ē, ǣ, eā, eō, u, o.

i (*continued*).

OLD.	MIDDLE.		MODERN.	
cliwe	cleu		*clew*	cluu
tiwes dæg	teuzdai	528	*Tuesday*	tyuuzdi
ifig	iivi		*ivy*	aivi
lifian	liv		*live*	liv
lifer	liver		*liver*	livər
sife	siv	532	*sieve*	siv
stīf	stif		*stiff*	stif
wifel	wiivil		*weevil*	wiivəl
gif	if		*if*	if
gifan	giv	536	*give*	giv
clif	clif		*cliff*	clif
drifen	driven		*driven*	drivən
siftan	sift		*sift*	sift
swift	swift	540	*swift*	swift
scrift	shrift		*shrift*	shrift
fīftig	fifti		*fifty*	fifti
gift	gift		*gift*	gift
hring	ring	544	*ring*	ring
-ling	-ling		*(dar)ling*	-ling
þing	þing		*thing*	þing
singan	sing		*sing*	sing
swingan	swing	548	*swing*	swing
stingan	sting		*sting*	sting
springan	spring		*spring*	spring
wǣng N. (vǣngr)	wing		*wing*	wing
finger	finger	552	*finger*	fingər
cringan	crinj		*cringe*	crinj
clingan	cling		*cling*	cling
bringan	bring		*bring*	bring
sincan	sinc	556	*sink*	sinc
slincan	slinc		*slink*	slinc
scrincan	shrinc		*shrink*	shrinc
stincan	stinc		*stink*	stinc
wincian	winc	560	*wink*	winc
drincan	drinc		*drink*	drinc
twinclian	twincl		*twinkle*	twincl
in(n)	in		*in(n)*	in
rinnan	run	564	*run*	rən
līn	linen		*linen*	linen

h; r, hr, l, hl; ð, s, w, hw, f; ng, n, m; g, c, d, t, b, p.

i (*continued*).

OLD.	MIDDLE.		MODERN.	
scin(bān)	shin		*shin*	shin
scinn N.	scin		*skin*	scin
spinnan	spin	568	*spin*	spin
gewinnan	win		*win*	win
windwian	winu		*winnow*	winóu
finn	fin		*fin*	fin
beginnan	begin	572	*begin*	begin
cinne	chin		*chin*	chin
tinn	tin		*tin*	tin
getwinnan	twinz		*twins*	twinz
binn	bin	576	*bin*	bin

hinde	hiind		*hind*	haind
hindema	hindermòòst		*hindermost*	hindermóust
rind	riind		*rind*	raind
lind	linden	580	*linden*	lindən
sinder	sinder		*cinder*	sindər
spindel	spindl		*spindle*	spindl
wind	wind		*wind*	wind
windan	wiind	584	*wind*	waind
windauga N.	windu		*window*	windóu
windwian (*under* n)				
findan	fiind		*find*	faind
grindan	griind		*grind*	graind
bindan	biind	588	*bind*	baind
blind	bliind		*blind*	blaind

stintan	stint		*stint*	stint
winter	winter		*winter*	wintər
flint	flint	592	*flint*	flint
minte	mint		*mint*	mint

---

him	him		*him*	him
rima	rim		*rim*	rim
lim	limb	596	*limb*	lim
swimman	swim		*swim*	swim
wīfman	wuman		*woman*	wumən
wīfmen	wumen (i)		*women*	wimen
grimm	grim	600	*grim*	grim
dimm	dim		*dim*	dim

climban	cliimb		*climb*	claim
timber	timber		*timber*	timbər

---

i (*continued*).

OLD.	MIDDLE.		MODERN.	
icgland	iiland	604	*island*	ailənd
higian	hii		*hie*	hai
licgan	lii		*lie*	lai
frigedæg	friidai		*Friday*	fraidi
nigon	niin	608	*nine*	nain
tigel	tiil		*tile*	tail
twig	twig		*twig*	twig
ic	ich, ii		*I*	ai
-līc	-li	612	(*like*)*ly*	-li
liccian	lic		*lick*	lic
þicce	þic		*thick*	þic
stician	stic		*stick*	stic
gestriccen	stricen	616	*stricken*	stricən
swi(l)c	such		*such*	səch
wicu	wiic		*week*	wiic
wicce	wich		*witch*	wich
hwi(l)c	which	620	*which*	which
ficol	ficl		*fickle*	ficl
flicce	flich		*flitch*	flich
micel	much		*much*	məch
gicel	(iis)icl	624	(*ic*)*icle*	(ais)icl
cwic	cwic		*quick*	cwic
bicce	bich		*bitch*	bich
pic	pich		*pitch*	pich
prician	pric	628	*prick*	pric
six	six		*six*	six
betwix	betwixt		*betwixt*	betwixt
hider	hiðer		*hither*	hiðər
riden	riden	632	*ridden*	ridn
hlid	lid		*lid*	lid
þider	ðiðer		*thither*	ðiðər
þridda (*under* r)				
widuwe	widu		*widow*	widóu
hwider	whiðer	636	*whither*	whiðər
biden	biden		*bidden*	bidn
bridd (*under* r)				
*wīð	widþ		*width*	width
tōmiddes	midst		*midst*	midst
hit	it	640	*it*	it
hitta N.	hit		*hit*	hit

h; r, hr, l, hl; ð, s, w, hw, f; ng, n, m; g, c, d, t, b, p.

i (*continued*).

OLD.	MIDDLE.		MODERN.	
sittan	sit		*sit*	sit
sliten / slītan	slit		*slit*	slit
smiten	smiten	644	*smitten*	smitn
gewitt / witan	wit		*wit*	wit
writen	writen		*written*	ritn
git	yit (e)		*yet*	yet
begitan	get	648	*get*	get
edwītan	twit		*twit*	twit
bite	bit		*bit*	bit
biter	biter		*bitter*	bitər

ribb	rib	652	*rib*	rib
sibb	(go)sip		*(gos)sip*	(go)sip
cribb	crib		*crib*	crib

lippa	lip		*lip*	lip
slīpan	slip	656	*slip*	slip
scip	ship		*ship*	ship
-scipe	-ship		*(wor)ship*	-ship
gripe	grip		*grip*	grip
clippa N.	clip	660	*clip*	clip

ī.

bī	bii		*by*	bai

gelīhtan (*under* i)

Īrland	iirland		*Ireland*	aiələnd
Īren	iiron		*iron*	aiən
scīr	(shiir)	664	*sheer*	shiər
wīr	wiir		*wire*	waiər

smīla N.	smiil		*smile*	smail
wīle	wiil		*wile*	wail
hwīl	whiil	668	*while*	whail
fīl	fiil		*file*	fail
mīl	miil		*mile*	mail

līðe	liið		*lithe*	laið
strīð	striif	672	*strife*	straif

a(æ ea ei), i, é(eo), è, ē, ǣ, eā, eō, u, o.

ī (*continued*).

OLD.	MIDDLE.		MODERN.	
wrīðan	wriið		*writhe*	raið
blīðe	bliið		*blithe*	blaið
īs	iis		*ice*	ais
arīsa	ariiz	676	*arise*	əraiz
wīs	wiiz		*wise*	waiz
wīsdōm	wizdom		*wisdom*	wizdəm
stīweard	steuard		*steward*	styuuəd
spīwan	speu	680	*spew*	spyuu
līf	liif		*life*	laif
þrīfan	þriiv		*thrive*	þraiv
scrīfan	shriiv		*shrive*	shraiv
stīf	stif	684	*stiff*	stif
wīf	wiif		*wife*	waif
fīf	fiiv		*five*	faiv
cnīf	cniif		*knife*	naif
drīfan	driiv	688	*drive*	draiv
wīfman (*under* im)				
fīftig	fifti		*fifty*	fifti
līn (*under* i)				
þīn	ðiin		*thine*	ðain
swīn	swiin		*swine*	swain
scīnan	shiin	692	*shine*	shain
scrīn	shriin		*shrine*	shrain
wīn	wiin		*wine*	wain
mīn	mii(n)		*mine, my*	mai(n)
twīn	twiin	696	*twine*	twain
pīnan	piin		*pine*	pain
rīm	riim		*rhyme*	raim
hrīm	riim		*rime*	raim
līm	liim	700	*lime*	laim
slīm	sliim		*slime*	slaim
wī(f)man (*under* im)				
tīma	tiim		*time*	taim
stīge	stii		*stye*	stai
stīgel	stiil	704	*stile*	stail
stīgrap	stirup		*stirrup*	stirəp

h; r, hr, l, hl; ð, s, w, hw, f; ng, n, m; g, c, d, t, b, p.

ī (*continued*).

OLD.	MIDDLE.		MODERN.	
mīgan	mii		*mie*	mii

rīce	rich		*rich*	rich
gelīc	liic	708	*like*	laic
-īc (*under* i)				
sīcan	siih		*sigh*	sai
snīcan	snèèk		*sneak*	sniic
strīcan	striic		*strike*	straic
dīc	diic	712	*dyke*	daic
	dich		*ditch*	dich

īdel	iidl		*idle*	aidl
rīdan	riid		*ride*	raid
sīde	siid	716	*side*	said
slīdan	sliid		*slide*	slaid
wīd	wiid		*wide*	waid
glīdan	gliid		*glide*	glaid
cīdan	chiid	720	*chide*	chaid
tīd	tiid		*tide*	taid
bīdan	biid		*bide*	baid
brīdels	briidl		*bridle*	braidl

slītan (*under* i)				
smītan	smiit	724	*smite*	smait
edwītan (*under* i)				
wrītan	wriit		*write*	rait
hwīt	whiit		*white*	whait
bītan	biit		*bite*	bait

rīpe	riip	728	*ripe*	raip
rīpan	rèèp		*reap*	riip
slīpan	slip		*slip*	slip
grīpan	griip		*gripe*	graip

y.

flyht	fliht	732	*flight*	flait
byht	biht		*bight*	bait

styrian	stir		*stir*	stəər
cyrice	church (i, y)		*church*	chəəch

a(æ ea ei), i, é(eo), è, ē, ǣ, eā, eō, u, o.

y (*continued*).

OLD.	MIDDLE.		MODERN.	
byrig	-byri	736	(*Canter*)*bury*	-bəri
wyrhta	wriht		*wright*	rait
þyrlian (*under* l)				
byrðen	burden		*burden*	bəədn
wyrsa	wurs		*worse*	wəəs
fyrs	furz	740	*furze*	fəəz
þyrstan	þirst		*thirst*	þəəst
fyrsta	first		*first*	fəəst
wyrm	wurm		*worm*	wəəm
bebyrgan	byri	744	*bury*	beri
wyrcan	wurc		*work*	wəəc
myrc	mirci		*mirky*	məəci
wyrd (*subs.*)	wiird		*wierd* (adj.)	wiəd
gebyrd	birþ	748	*birth*	bəəþ
scyrta N. {	skirt		*skirt*	skəət
	shirt		*shirt*	shəət
wyrt	wurt		*wort*	wəət
? yfel (*see* ill)	il	752	*ill*	il
hyll	hil		*hill*	hil
þyrlian	þril		*thrill*	þril
syll	sil		*sill*	sil
mylen	mil	756	*mill*	mil
fyllan	fil		*fill*	fil
bylgja N.	bilu		*billow*	bilóu
fȳlð	filþ		*filth*	filþ
gyldan	gild	760	*gild*	gild
byldan	byld (i)		*build*	bild
gylt	gilt		*guilt*	gilt
cȳðð	ciþ		*kith* (*and kin*)	ciþ

h; r, hr, l, hl; ð, s, w, hw, f; ng, n, m; g, c, d, t, b, p.

y (*continued*).

OLD.	MIDDLE.		MODERN.	
cyssan	cis	764	*kiss*	cis
bysig	byzi		*busy*	bizi
wȳscan	wish		*wish*	wish
lystan	list		*list(less)*	list
fȳst	fist	768	*fist*	fist
clyster	cluster		*cluster*	cləstər
treysta N.	tryst (u)		*trust*	trəst
yfel	? èèvel		*evil*	iivl
lyftan	lift	772	*lift*	lift
cyng	cing		*king*	cing
ynce	inch		*inch*	inch
þyncan	þinc		*think*	þinc
þynne	þin	776	*thin*	þin
synn	sin		*sin*	sin
cynn	cin		*kin*	cin
cyning (*under* ng)				
dyne	din		*din*	din
mynster	minster	780	*minster*	minstər
gemynd	miind		*mind*	maind
gecynde	ciind		*kind*	caind
tynder	tinder		*tinder*	tindər
byndel	bundl	784	*bundle*	bəndl
mynet	mint		*mint*	mint
dynt	dint		*dint*	dint
trymman	trim		*trim*	trim
cymlic	cumli	788	*comely*	cəmli
hrycg	rij		*ridge*	rij
lyge	lii		*lie*	lai
flycge (*adj.*)	flejd		*fledged*	flejd
mycg	mij	792	*mij*	mij

a(æ ea ei), i, é(eo), è, ē, ǣ, eā, eō, u, o.

y (*continued*).

OLD.	MIDDLE.		MODERN.	
drygo	drii		*dry*	drai
bycgan	byy		*buy*	bai
brycg	brij		*bridge*	brij
? lycci N.	luc	796	*luck*	ləc
mycel	much (i)		*much*	məch
cycen	chicen		*chicken*	chicen
cycene	cichen	800	*kitchen*	cichen
crycc	cruch		*crutch*	crəch
fyxen	vixen		*vixen*	vixən
gehȳded	hid		*hid*	hid
dyde	did	804	*did*	did
lytel	litl		*little*	litl
scytel	shutl		*shuttle*	shətl
scyttan	shut (i)		*shut*	shət
spyttan	spit	808	*spit*	spit
flytja N.	flit		*flit*	flit
cnyttan	cnit		*knit*	nit
pytt	pit		*pit*	pit
clyppan	clip	812	*clip*	clip
dyppan	dip		*dip*	dip

ȳ.

scȳ N.	skii		*sky*	skai
hwȳ	whii		*why*	whai
cȳ	cii	816	*kye*	cai
ahȳrian	hiir		*hire*	haiər
fȳr	fiir		*fire*	faiər
gefȳlan	fiil		*(de)file*	fail
fȳlð (*under* y)				
hȳð	hiið	820	*hithe*	haið

h; r, hr, l, hl; ð, s, w, hw, f; ng, n, m; g, c, d, t, b, p.

y (*continued*).

OLD.	MIDDLE.		MODERN.	
cȳðð (*under* y)				
lȳs	liis		*lice*	lais
mȳs	miis		*mice*	mais
fȳst (*under* y)				
wȳscan (*under* y)				
hȳd	hiid		*hide*	haid
hȳdan	hiid	824	*hide*	haid
brȳd	briid		*bride*	braid
prȳte	priid		*pride*	praid

é, eo.

þe (=se)	ðe		*the*	ðe, ðə
? bleoh (=*blue*)				
leōht	liht	828	*light*	lait
feohtan	fiht		*fight*	fait
smerian	smèèr		*smear*	smiər
sceran	shèèr		*shear*	shiər
steorra	star	832	*star*	star
spere	spèèr		*spear*	spiər
feorr	far		*far*	far
merg (*adj.*)	meri		*merry*	meri
teran	tèèr	836	*tear*	tèər
teru	tar		*tar*	tar
beran / bera	bèèr		*bear*	bèər
beorht (*see* briht)				
merhð	mirþ		*mirth*	moəþ
eorðe	èèrþ	840	*earth*	əəþ
heorð	hèèrþ		*hearth*	haəþ
weorð	wurþ		*worth*	wəəþ
feorðling	farðing		*farthing*	faəðing
*dērð	dèèrþ	844	*dearth*	dəəþ

a(æ ea ei), i, é(eo), è, ē, ǣ, eā, eō, u, o.

é, eo (*continued*).

OLD.	MIDDLE.		MODERN.	
eorl	èèrl		*earl*	əəl
ceorl	churl		*churl*	chəəl
cerse (*under* s)				
þerscan	þrash		*thrash*	þræsh
fersc (*under* sc)				
berstan	burst	848	*burst*	bəəst
ceorfan	carv		*carve*	caəv
sweorfan	swerv		*swerve*	swəəv
steorfan	starv		*starve*	staəv
eornan	run	852	*run*	rən
eornost	èèrnest		*earnest*	əənest
leornian	lèèrn		*learn*	ləən
speornan	spurn		*spurn*	spəən
gernan	yèèrn	856	*yearn*	yəən
beornan	burn		*burn*	bəən
beorma	barm		*barm*	baəm
dweorg	dwarf		*dwarf*	dwòəf
beorg	? (iis)berg	860	(*ice*)*berg*	(ais)bəəg
	baru		*barrow*	bæróu
weorc	wurc		*work*	wəəc
deorc	darc		*dark*	daəc
beorce	birch	864	*birch*	bəəch
beorcan	barc		*bark*	baəc
hērenian	harc		*hark*	haəc
	hèèrcen		*hearken*	haəcen
sweord	swurd	868	*sword*	sòòəd
heort	hart		*hart*	hart
heorte	hèèrt		*heart*	hart
swellan	swel		*swell*	swel
smella N.	smel	872	*smell*	smel
stelan	stèèl		*steal*	stiil
spellian	spel		*spell*	spel
wel	wel		*well*	wel
wela	wèèl	876	*weal*	wiil
fell	fel		*fell*	fel

é, eo (*continued*).

OLD.	MIDDLE.		MODERN.	
fēlagi N.	felu		*fellow*	felóu
melu	mèèl		*meal*	miil
geolo	yelu	880	*yellow*	yelóu
cwelan	cwail		*quail*	cwéil
belle	bel		*bell*	bel
seolh	sèèl		*seal*	siil
self	self	884	*self*	self
seolfor	silver		*silver*	silvər
delfan	delv		*delve*	delv
twelf	twelv		*twelve*	twelv
elm	elm	888	*elm*	elm
helm	helm		*helm*	helm
swelgan	swalu		*swallow*	swolóu
belgan	belu		*bellow*	belóu
seoloc	silc	892	*silk*	silc
weoloc	whelc		*whelk*	whelc
meolc	milc		*milk*	milc
geolca	yolc		*yolk*	yóuc
heōld (*pret.*)	held	896	*held*	held
seldon	seldom		*seldom*	seldəm
feld	fiild		*field*	fiild
smeltan	smelt		*smelt*	smelt
gefēled	felt	900	*felt*	felt
meltan	melt		*melt*	melt
helpan	help		*help*	help
gelpan	yelp		*yelp*	yelp
leðer	lèèðer	904	*leather*	leðər
weðer	weðer		*wether*	weðer
beneoðan	benèèþ		*beneath*	beniiþ
brēðer	breðren		*brethren*	breðren
cerse	cres	908	*cress*	cres
blētsian	bles		*bless*	bles
wesle	wèèzəl		*weasel*	wiizl
besma	bezom		*besom*	bezəm

a(æ ea ei), i, é(eo), è, ē, ǣ, eā, eō, u, o.

é, eo (*continued*).

OLD.	MIDDLE.		MODERN.	
þrescan	þresh	912	*thresh*	þræsh
fersc	fresh		*fresh*	fresh
sweostor	sister		*sister*	sistər
nest	nest		*nest*	nest
cest	chest	916	*chest*	chest
efen	èèven		*even*	iivn
heofon	hèèven		*heaven*	hevn
seofan	seven		*seven*	sevn
wefan	wèèv	920	*weave*	wiiv
fefer	fèèver		*fever*	fiivər
þēfð	þeft		*theft*	þeft
hēng	hung		*hung*	hung
tēn	ten	924	*ten*	ten
begeondan	beyond		*beyond*	beyond
eom (*see* eam)				
brēmel	brambl		*bramble*	bræmbl
weg	wai		*way*	wéi
be(de)gian	beg	928	*beg*	beg
plega	plai		*play*	pléi
leg(e)r	lair		*lair*	lèèər
seg(e)l	sail		*sail*	séil
reg(e)n	rain	932	*rain*	réin
geleg(e)n	lain		*lain*	léin
þeg(e)n	þaan		*thane*	þéin
tweg(e)n	twain		*twain*	twéin
breg(e)n	brain	936	*brain*	bréin
? blegen	blain		*(chill)blain*	bléin
bregdan	braid		*braid*	bréid
sprecan	spèèc		*speak*	spiic
wrecan	wrèèc	940	*wreak*	rec
brecan	brèèc		*break*	bréic

é, eo (*continued*).

OLD.	MIDDLE.		MODERN.	
nēxt	next		*next*	next
bēcnian	becon		*beckon*	becən
weder	wèèðer	944	*weather*	weðər
fēded	fed		*fed*	fed
medu	mèèd		*mead*	miid
cnedan	cnèèd		*knead*	niid
tredan	trèèd	948	*tread*	tred
gebed	bèèd		*bead*	biid
brēded	bred		*bred*	bred
blēded	bled		*bled*	bled
etan	èèt	952	*eat*	iit
lēt (*pret.*)	let		*let*	let
fetor	feter		*fetter*	fetər
setlian	setl		*settle*	setl
nebb	nib	956	*nib*	nib
scǣphirde	shepherd		*shepherd*	shepəd
*dēpð	depþ		*depth*	depþ
pepor	peper		*pepper*	pepər
slǣpte	slept	960	*slept*	slept

è

èrian	èèr		*ear*	iər
swèrian	swèèr		*swear*	swèər
wèrian	wèèr		*wear*	wèər
mère (*sm.*)	mèèr	964	*mere*	miər
mère (*sf.*)	maar		*mare*	mèər
mèrran	mar		*mar*	maar
bère	bar-		*bar-ley*	baəli
bèrige	beri	968	*berry*	beri
ǣr(e)st	erst		*erst*	əəst
mèrsc	marsh		*marsh*	maəsh

a(æ ea ei), i, é(eo), è, ē, ǣ, eā, eō, u, o.

è (*continued*).

OLD.	MIDDLE.		MODERN.	
hèrwe	haru		*harrow*	hærou
bèrn(=bère-ærn)	barn	972	*barn*	baən
smèrcian	smirc		*smirk*	sməɔc
gèrd	yard		*yard*	yaɔd
gèrdels	girdl		*girdle*	gəədl
begèrded	girt	976	*girt*	gəət
è(nd)lufon	eleven		*eleven*	elevən
hèll	hel		*hell*	hel
sèllan	sel		*sell*	sel
gesǣlig	sili	980	*silly*	sili
scèll	shel		*shell*	shel
wèll	wel		*well*	wel
fèllan	fel		*fell*	fel
cwèllan {	cwel	984	*quell*	cwel
	cil		*kill*	cil
dwèlja N.	dwel		*dwell*	dwel
tèllan	tel		*tell*	tel
èlles	els	988	*else*	els
wèlsc	welsh		*Welsh*	welsh
scèlfe	shelf		*shelf*	shelf
èln	el		*ell*	el
tèlg	talu	992	*tallow*	tælou
bèlg {	beluz		*bellows*	belóuz
	beli		*belly*	beli
èldest	eldest		*eldest*	eldest
gewèldan	wiild	996	*wield*	wiild
gèlda N.	geld		*geld*	geld
bèlt	belt		*belt*	belt
hwèlp	whelp		*whelp*	whelp
flǣsc	flesh	1000	*flesh*	flesh

h; r, hr, l, hl; ð, s, w, hw, f; ng, n, m; g, c, d, t, b, p.

è (*continued*).

OLD.	MIDDLE.		MODERN.	
behǣs	behest		*behest*	behest
wrǣstan	wrest		*wrest*	rest
gèst	gest		*guest*	gest
bè(t)st	best	1004	*best*	best
wèsp	wasp		*wasp*	wosp

ǣfre	ever		*ever*	evər
èfese	èèvz		*eaves*	iivz
(ic) hèfe	hèèv	1008	*heave*	hiiv
hèfig	hèèvi		*heavy*	hevi
èft	eft		*eft(soons)*	eft
bereāfod	bereft		*bereft*	bereft
gelǣfed	left	1012	*left*	left

ðǣm	ðem		*them*	ðem
stèmn	stem		*stem*	stem

èngland	england		*England*	inglənd
ènglisc	english	1016	*English*	inglish
sèngan	sinj		*singe*	sinj
*lèngð	lengþ		*length*	lengþ
strèngðo	strengþ		*strength*	strengþ
hlènce	linc	1020	*link*	linc
þèncan (*see* þyncan)				
stènc	stench		*stench*	stench
wèncle	wench		*wench*	wench
frèncisc	french		*French*	french
cwèncan	cwench	1024	*quench*	cwench
drèncan	drench		*drench*	drench
bènc	bench		*bench*	bench

hènne	hen		*hen*	hen
lǣnan	lend	1028	*lend*	lend
wènian	wèèn		*wean*	wiin
wènn	wen		*wen*	wen
fènn	fen		*fen*	fen
mènn	men	1032	*men*	men
cènnan	cen		*ken*	cen
dènn	den		*den*	den

è (*continued*).

OLD.	MIDDLE.			MODERN.
pèning	peni		*penny*	peni
clǣnsian	?clènz	1036	*cleanse*	clenz
ènde	end		*end*	end
gehènde	handi		†*handy*	hændi
hrèndan	rend		*rend*	rend
sèndan	send	1040	*send*	send
spèndan	spend		*spend*	spend
wèndan	wend		*wend*	wend
bèndan	bend		*bend*	bend
blèndan	blend	1044	*blend*	blend
hrènded	rent		*rent*	rent
lèn(c)ten	lent		*lent*	lent
sended	sent		*sent*	sent
spènded	spent	1048	*spent*	spent
wènded	went		*went*	went
bènded	bent		*bent*	bent
ǣmyrie	emberz		*embers*	embəəz
tèmese	(temz)	1052	*Thames*	temz
èmtig	empti		*empty*	em(p)ti
ège	au		*awe*	òò
ècg	ej		*edge*	ej
ègg N.	eg	1056	*egg*	eg
hège	hej		*hedge*	hej
lècgan	lai		*lay*	léi
lègg N.	leg		*leg*	leg
sècgan	sai	1060	*say*	séi
sècg	sej		*sedge*	sej
wècg	wej		*wedge*	wej
èglan	ail		*ail*	éil
èce	aach	1064	*ache*	éic
rècenian	recon		*reckon*	recən
hlèce (*adj.*)	lèèc		*leak*	liic
strèccan	strech		*stretch*	strech
wrècca	wrech	1068	*wretch*	rech
fèccan	fech		*fetch*	fech
hnècca	nec		*neck*	nec

h; r, hr, l, hl; ð, s, w, hw, f; ng, n, m; g, c, d, t, b, p.

è (*continued*).

OLD.	MIDDLE.			MODERN
ahrèddan	rid		*rid*	rid
gelǣded	led	1072	*led*	led
stède	stèèd		*stead*	sted
wèdd	wed		*to wed*	wed
bèdd	bed		*bed*	bed
lèttan lǣtan	let	1076	*let*	let
sèttan gesèted	set		*set*	set
wǣt (*adj.*)	wet		*wet*	wet
hwèttan	whet		*whet*	whet
nètt	net	1080	*net*	net
nètele	netl		*nettle*	netl
mète	mèèt		*meat*	miit
cètel	cetl		*kettle*	cetl
bètera	beter	1084	*better*	betər
èbbian	eb		*ebb*	eb
wèbb	web		*web*	web
nèbb	nib		*nib*	nib
stèppan	step	1088	*step*	step

ē.

hē	héé		*he*	hii
þē	ðéé		*th*	ðii
wē	wéé		*we*	wii
mē	méé	1092	*me*	mii
gē	yéé		*ye*	yii
hēh	hiih		*high*	hai
nēh	niih		*nigh*	nai
hēr	héér	1096	*here*	hiər
gehēran	? hèèr (éé)		*hear*	hiər
wērig	? wèèri (éé)		*weary*	wiəri
hērenian	hèèrcen		*hearken*	haəcən

a(æ ea ei), i, é(eo), è, ē, ǣ, eā, eō, u, o.

ē (*continued*).

OLD.	MIDDLE.		MODERN.	
gehērde	hèèrd	1100	*heard*	həəd
hēl	héél		*heel*	hiil
stēl	stéél		*steel*	stiil
fēlan	fééł		*feel*	fiil
cēle	chil	1104	*chill*	chil
? cnēla N.	cnéél		*kneel*	niil
smēðe (*under* ō)				
tēð	tééþ		*teeth*	tiiþ
brēðer (*under* é)				
gelēfan	beléév		*believe*	beliiv
slēfe	sléév	1108	*sleeve*	sliiv
dēfan	diiv		*dive*	daiv
þēfð (*under* é)				
hēng (*pret.*) (*under* ó)				
scēne	shéén		*sheen*	shiin
wēnan	wéén	1112	*ween*	wiin
grēne	gréén		*green*	griin
cēne	céén		*keen*	ciin
cwēn	cwéén		*queen*	cwiin
tēn	ten	1116	*ten*	ten
þreōtēne	þirtéén		*thirteen*	þəətiin
bēn (*under* ō)				
gesēman	séém		*seem*	siim
dēman	déém		*deem*	diim
tēman	téém	1120	*teem*	tiim
brēmel (*under* ó)				
ēge (=eā)	ei, ii		*eye*	ai
hēg	hai		*hay*	héi
slœ̄g N.	slii		*sly*	slai
tēgan	tii	1124	*tie*	tai
ēcan	ééc		*eke*	iic
rēc (=eā)	réééc		*reek*	riic
hrēc (=eā)	ric		*rick*	ric
rēcan	rec	1128	*reck*	rec
lēc (=eā)	lééc		*leek*	liic

h; r, hr, l, hl; ð, s, w, hw, f; ng, n, m; g, c, d, t, b, p.

ē (*continued*).

OLD.	MIDDLE.		MODERN.	
sēcan	sééc		*seek*	siic
cēc (=eā)	chééc		*cheek*	chiic
bēce	béééch	1132	*beech*	biich
brēc	brééch		*breech*	briich
nēxt (*under* é)				
bēcnian (*under* é)				
hēdan	héééd		*heed*	hiid
rēdan	rèèd (éé)		*read*	riid
stēda	stééd	1136	*steed*	stiid
spēd	spééd		*speed*	spiid
fēdan	fééd		*feed*	fiid
fēded (*under* é)				
nēd	nééd		*need*	niid
mēd	mééd	1140	*meed*	miid
glēd	gléééd		*gleed*	gliid
crēda	crééd		*creed*	criid
brēdan	bréééd		*breed*	briid
blēdan	bléééd	1144	*bleed*	bliid
lēt (*under* é)				
swēte	swéét		*sweet*	swiit
scēt (=eā)	shéét		*sheet*	shiit
fēt	féét		*feet*	fiit
gemētan	méét	1148	*meet*	miit
grētan	gréét		*greet*	griit
bētel	béétl		*beetle*	biitl
blētsian (*under* é)				
stēp (=eā)	stéép		*steep*	stiip
stēpel	stéépl	1152	*steeple*	stiipl
wēpan	wéép		*weep*	wiip
cēpan	céép		*keep*	ciip
crēpel	cripl		*cripple*	cripl
dēpan (*see* dyppan)	dip	1156	*dip*	dip
*dēpð (*under* é)				

ǣ = (éé).

OLD.	MIDDLE.		MODERN.	
hǣr	? hair		*hair*	hèər
þǣr	ðèèr		*there*	ðèər
wǣron	wèèr		*were*	wèər
hwǣr	whèèr	1160	*where*	whèər
fǣr	fèèr		*fear*	fiər
bǣr	? béér		*bier*	biər
ǣl	éél		*eel*	iil
? gesǣlig	sili	1164	*silly*	sili
mǣl	mèèl		*meal*	miil
brǣð	brèèþ		*breath*	breþ
*brǣðan	brèèð		*breathe*	briið
cǣse	chééz	1168	*cheese*	chiiz
ǣfen	èèven		*even*	iivn
ǣmette (*under* a)				
wǣg	waav		*wave*	wéiv
wǣgan	weih		*weigh*	wéi
hwǣg	whei	1172	*whey*	whéi
hnǣgan	neih		*neigh*	néi
grǣg	grai, grei		*gray, grey*	gréi
cǣge	cei		*key*	cii
*wǣgð	weiht	1176	*weight*	wéit
lǣce	léćch		*leech*	liich
sprǣc	spééch		*speech*	spiich
þrǣd	þrèèd		*thread*	þred
wǣd	wéédz	1180	*weeds*	wiidz
sǣd	sééd		*seed*	siid
grǣdig	grééidi		*greedy*	griidi
dǣd	dééd		*deed*	diid
ondrǣdan	drèèd	1184	*dread*	dred
nǣdl	néédl		*needle*	niidl
lǣtan (*under* è)				
strǣt	strééet		*street*	striit
wǣt (*under* è)				

h; r, hr, l, hl; ð, s, w, hw, f; ng, n, m; g, c, d, t, b, p.

ǣ(=éé) (*continued*).

OLD.	MIDDLE.			MODERN.
blǣtan	blèèt	1188	*bleat*	bliit
slǣp	sléép		*sleep*	sliip
swǣpan	swéép		*sweep*	swiip
scǣp	shéép		*sheep*	shiip
wǣpen	wèèpon	1192	*weapon*	wepən
slǣpte (*under* é)				

ǣ(=èè).

OLD.	MIDDLE.			MODERN.
sǣ	sèè		*sea*	sii
tǣhte (*under* a)				
ǣr	èèr		*ere*	èèər
rǣran	rèèr		*rear*	riər
ǣrest (*under* è)				
hǣlan	hèèl	1196	*heal*	hiil
þrǣl N.	þral		*thrall*	þròòl
dǣl	dèèl		*deal*	diil
hǣlð	? hèèlþ		*health*	helþ
ǣlc (*under* c)				
hǣðen	hèèðen	1200	*heathen*	hiiðən
scǣð	shèèþ		*sheath*	shiiþ
wrǣð	wrèèþ		*wreath*	riiþ
? brǣð	brèèþ		*breath*	breþ
? brǣðan	brèèð	1204	*breathe*	briið
behǣs (*under* è)				
tǣsan	tèèz		*tease*	tiiz
flǣsc (*under* è)				

a(æ ea ei), i, é(eo), è, ē, ǣ, eā, eō, u, o.

ǣ(=èè) (*continued*).

OLD.	MIDDLE.		MODERN.	
lǣstan (*under* a)				
wrǣstan (*under* è)				
lǣwed	leud		*lewd*	lyuud
lǣfan	lèèv		*leave*	liiv
hlǣfdige (*under* a)				
ǣfre (*under* è)				
gelǣfed (*under* è)				
ǣnig (*under* a)				
lǣnan (*under* è)				
hlǣne	lèèn	1208	*lean*	liin
clǣne	clèèn		*clean*	cliin
mǣnan	mèèn		*mean*	miin
gemǣne	mèèn		*mean*	miin
ǣmyric (*under* è)				
þǣm (*under* è)				
clǣg	clai	1212	*clay*	cléi
ǣ(l)c	èèch		*each*	iich
rǣcan	rèèch		*reach*	riich
tǣcan	tèèch		*teach*	tiich
blǣc(=ā)	blèèc	1216	*bleak*	bliic
blǣcan	blèèch		*bleach*	bliich
rǣdan	rèèd		*read*	riid
lǣdan	lèèd		*lead*	liid
gelǣded (*under* è)				
*brǣdð	brèèdþ	1220	*breadth*	bredþ
hǣto	hèèt		*heat*	hiit
sǣti N.	sèèt		*seat*	siit
swǣt	swèèt		*sweat*	swet
spǣtte (*under* a)				
hwǣte	whèèt	1224	*wheat*	whiit
wǣt (*under* è)				
fǣtt (*under* a)				

h; r, hr, l, hl; ð, s, w, hw, f; ng, n, m; g, c, d, t, b, p.

eā.

OLD.	MIDDLE.		MODERN.	
fleā	flèè		*flea*	flii
geā	yèè		*yea*	yéi
ceā	? chuuh		*chough*	chəf
þeāh	ðòòuh	1228	*though*	ðóu
eāre	èèr		*ear*	iər
forseārian	sèèr		*sear*	siər
neār	nèèr		*near*	niər
geār	yèèr	1232	*year*	yiər
teār	tèèr		*tear*	tiər
deāð	dèèþ		*death*	deþ
ceās	chòòz		*chose*	chóuz
eāst	èèst	1236	*east*	iist
eāstre	èèster		*easter*	iistər
heāwan	heu		*hew*	hyuu
hreāw	rau		*raw*	ròò
þeāw	þeu	1240	*thew*	þyuu
sleāw	slòòu		*slow*	slóu
sceāwian	shòòu (eu)		*show* (*shew*)	shóu
screāwa	shreu		*shrew*	shruu
streāw	strau	1244	*straw*	stròò
streāwian	streu		*strew*	struu
feāwa	feu		*few*	fyuu
deāw	deu		*dew*	dyuu
breāw (*see* brū)				
heāfod (*under* d)				
bereāfian	berèèv	1248	*bereave*	beriiv
leāf	lèèf		*leaf*	liif
sceāf	shèèf		*sheaf*	shiif
deāf	dèèf		*deaf*	def
beān	bèèn	1252	*bean*	biin
seām	sèèm		*seam*	siim
steām	stèèm		*steam*	stiim
streām	strèèm		*stream*	striim
gleām	glèèm	1256	*gleam*	gliim
dreām	drèèm		*dream*	driim

a(æ ea ei), i, é(eo), è, ē, ǣ, eā, eō, u, o.

eā (*continued*).

OLD.	MIDDLE.		MODERN.	
teām	tèèm		*team*	tiim
beām	bèèm		*beam*	biim
eāge (*under* ē)				
fleāg	fleu	1260	*flew*	fluu
hreāc (*under* ē)				
leāc (*under* ē)				
ceāc (*under* ē)				
beācen	bèècon		*beacon*	biicən
heā(fo)d	hèèd		*head*	hed
reād	rèèd		*red*	red
leād	lèèd	1264	*lead*	led
sceādan	shed		*shed*	shed
screādian	shred		*shred*	shred
neād (*under* ē)				
deād	dèèd		*dead*	ded
breād	brèèd	1268	*bread*	bred
sceāt (*under* ē)				
sceāt (*pret.*)	†shot		*shot*	shot
neāt	nèèt		*neat*	niit
greāt	grèèt		*great*	gréit
beātan	bèèt	1272	*beat*	biit
heāp	hèèp		*heap*	hiip
hleāpan	hlèèp		*leap*	liip
steāp (*under* ē)				
ceāp (*subs.*)	chèèp (*adj.*)		*cheap*	chiip
ceāpman	chapman	1276	*chapman*	chæpmən
creāp (*pret.*)	†crept		*crept*	crept

eō.

þreō	þréé		*three*	þrii
seōn (*vb.*)	séé		*see*	sii
seō	shéé	1280	*she*	shii
feō(h)	féé		*fee*	fii

h ; r, hr, l, hl ; ð, s, w, hw, f ; ng, n, m ; g, c, d, t, b, p.

eō (*continued*).

OLD.	MIDDLE.		MODERN.	
freō	frée		*free*	frii
fleō	flée		*flee*	flii
gleō	glée	1284	*glee*	glii
beō (*vb.*)	bée		*be*	bii
beō (*subs.*)	bée		*bee*	bii
þeōh	þiih		*thigh*	þai
hreōh	ruuh	1288	*rough*	rəf
leōht (*under* é)				
hleōr	léér		*leer*	liər
deōr	déér		*deer*	diər
deōre	dèèr (éé)		*dear*	diər
deōrling	darling	1292	*darling*	daəling
dreōrig	drèèri		*dreary*	driəri
beōr	béér		*beer*	biər
feōrða	fourþ		*fourth*	fòəþ
hweōl	whéél	1296	*wheel*	whiil
? geōl	?		*yule*	yuul
ceōl	céél		*keel*	ciil
heōld (*under* é)				
seōðan	sééð		*seethe*	siið
geō(g)uð	yuuþ	1300	*youth*	yuuþ
forleōsan	(lóóz)		*lose*	luuz
freōsan	fréez		*freeze*	friiz
fleōse	flées		*fleece*	fliis
ceōsan	chóóz	1304	*choose*	chuuz
breōst	brèèst		*breast*	brest
eōw (*pron.*)	yuu		*you*	yuu
eōw	yeu		*yew*	yuu
eōwe	eu	1308	*ewe*	yuu
hreōwan	reu		*rue* (*rew*)	ruu
seōwian	seu		*sew*	sóu
hleōw	léé		*lee*	lii
feōwer	four	1312	*four*	fòər

eō (*continued*).

OLD.	MIDDLE.		MODERN.	
feōwertig	forti		*forty*	fòəti
greōw (*pret.*)	greu		*grew*	gruu
ceōwan	cheu		*chew*	chuu
creōw (*pret.*)	creu	1316	*crew*	cruu
cneōw (*pret.*)	cneu		*knew*	nyuu
cneōw (*subs.*)	cnéé		*knee*	nii
treōw	tréé		*tree*	trii
treōwe	treu	1320	*true* (*trew*)	truu
breōwan	breu		*brew*	bruu
bleōw (*pret.*)	bleu		*blew*	bluu
hreōwð	ryyþ		*ruth*	ruuþ
treōwð	tryyþ	1324	*truth*	truuþ
leōf	(lééf)		*lief*	liif
þeōf	(þééf)		*thief*	þiif
cleōfan	clèèv		*cleave*	cliiv
deōfol	devil	1328	*devil*	devl
geōng	yung		*young*	yəng
betweōnan	betwéén		*between*	betwiin
*gebeōn (*partic.*)	béén		*been*	biin
feōnd	(féénd)	1332	*fiend*	fiind
freōnd	(fréénd)		*friend*	frend
miūc N.	méée		*meek*	miic
leōgan	lii		*lie*	lai
fleōga	flii	1336	*fly*	flai
geōguð	yuuþ		*youth*	yuuþ
hreōd	rééd		*reed*	riid
weōd	wééd		*weed*	wiid
neōd	nééd	1340	*need*	niid
beōdan	bid		*bid*	bid
sceōtan	shóót		*shoot*	shuut
fleōt	fléét		*fleet*	fliit
beōt (*part.*)	beet	1344	*beat*	biit
heōp (*rose*)	hip		*hip*	hip

h; r, hr, l, hl; ð, s, w, hw, f; ng, n, m; g, c, d, t, b, p.

eō (*continued*).

OLD.	MIDDLE.		MODERN.	
hleōp (*pret.*)	†lept		*lept*	lept
sweōp (*pret.*)	†swept		*swept*	swept
weōp (*pret.*)	†wept	1348	*wept*	wept
creōpan	créép		*creep*	criip
deōp	déép		*deep*	diip

u

duru	(duur)		*door*	dòòr
þurh	þruuh	1352	*through*	þruu
	þoruh		*thorough*	þərə
furh	furu		*furrow*	fəróu
crulla N.	curl		*curl*	cəəl
wurð	wurþ	1356	*worth*	wəəþ
furðor	furðer		*further*	fəəðər
þunresdæg	þursdai		*Thursday*	þəəzdi
curs	curs		*curse*	cəəs
turf	turf	1360	*turf*	təəf
murnian	muurn		*mourn*	mòən
wurm	wurm		*worm*	wəəm
burg	? boru		*borough*	bərə
wurcan	wurc	1364	*work*	wəəc
swurd	swurd		*sword*	sòəd
wull	? wuul (u)		*wool*	wul
full	full		*full*	ful
crulla (*under* r)				
bulluca	buloc	1368	*bullock*	buləc

a(æ ea ei), i, é(eo), è, ē, ǣ, eā, eō, u, o.

u (*continued*).

OLD.	MIDDLE.		MODERN.	
wulf	wulf		*wolf*	wulf
sculdor	shuulder		*shoulder*	shóuldər
ūs	us		*us*	əs
hūsbōnda	huzband	1372	*husband*	həzbənd
tusc	tusc		*tusk*	təsc
būa sic N.	busc		*busk*	bəsc
rust	rust		*rust*	rəst
lust	lust	1376	*lust*	ləst
gust N.	gust		*gust*	gəst
dust	dust		*dust*	dəst
lufu	luv		*love*	ləv
èndlufon	eleven	1380	*eleven*	elevən
scūfan	shuv		*shove*	shəv
dūfe	duv		*dove*	dəv
ònbūfan	abuv		*above*	əbəv
hungor	hunger	1384	*hunger*	həngər
sungen	sung		*sung*	səng
wrungen	wrung		*wrung*	rəng
clungen	clung		*clung*	cləng
tunge	tung	1388	*tongue*	təng
munuc	munc		*monk*	mənc
druncen	drunc		*drunk*	drənc
hunig	huni		*honey*	həni
þunor	þunder	1392	*thunder*	þəndər
sunu	sun		*son*	sən
sunne	sun		*sun*	sən
scūnian	shun		*shun*	shən
spunnen	spun	1396	*spun*	spən
gewunnen	wun		*won*	wən
nunne	nun		*nun*	nən
munuc (*under* nc)				
cunnan	cuning		*cunning*	cəning
dunn	dun	1400	*dun*	dən
tunne	tun		*tun*	tən
under	under		*under*	əndər

h; r, hr, l, hl; ð, s, w, hw, f; ng, n, m; g, c, d, t, b, p.

u (*continued*).

OLD.	MIDDLE.		MODERN.	
hund	huund		*hound*	haund
hundred	hundred	1404	*hundred*	həndred
sund (*subs.*) / gesund (*adj.*)	suund		*sound*	saund
sundor	sunder		*sunder*	səndər
wund	wuund		*wound*	wuund
gewunden	wuund	1408	*wound*	waund
wundor	wunder		*wonder*	wəndər
funden	fuund		*found*	faund
grund	gruund		*ground*	graund
grunden	gruund	1412	*ground*	graund
bunden	buund		*bound*	baund
pund	puund		*pound*	paund
huntian	hunt		*hunt*	hənt
stunt (*adj.*)	stunt	1416	*to stunt*	stənt
? munt	muunt		*mount*	maunt
þūma	þumb		*thumb*	þəm
sum	sum		*some*	səm
sumor	sumer	1420	*summer*	səmər
swummen	swum		*swum*	swəm
slumerian	slumber		*slumber*	sləmbər
guma	gruum		*groom*	gru(u)m
cuman	cum	1424	*come*	cəm
crume	crumb		*crumb*	crəm
dumb	dumb		*dumb*	dəm
ugglig N.	ugli		*ugly*	əgli
sugu	suu	1428	*sow*	sau
fugol	fuul		*fowl*	faul
cnucian	cnoc		*knock*	noc
cnucel	cnucl		*knuckle*	nəcl
bucca	buc	1432	*buck*	bəc
pluccian	pluc		*pluck*	pləc
wudu	? wuud (u)		*wood*	wud
hnutu	nut		*nut*	nət
gutt	gut	1436	*gut*	gət

u (*continued*).

OLD.	MIDDLE.		MODERN.	
būton	but		*but*	bət
butere	buter		*butter*	bətər
? putta N.	put		*put*	put
upp	up	1440	*up*	əp
hup	hip		*hip*	hip
sūpan	sup		*sup*	səp
cuppa	cup		*cup*	cəp

ū.

hū	huu	1444	*how*	hau
ðū	ðuu		*thou*	ðau
nū	nuu		*now*	nau
cū	cuu		*cow*	cau
brū	bruu	1448	*brow*	brau
ūre	uur		*our*	auər
sūr	suur		*sour*	sauər
scūr	shuuer		*shower*	shauər
būr	buuer	1452	*bower*	bauər
gebūr	(buur)		*boor*	buər
(neāh)gebūr	(neih)buur		*(neigh)bour*	(néi)bər
ūle	uul		*owl*	aul
fūl	fuul	1456	*foul*	faul
sūð	suuþ		*south*	sauþ
mūð	muuþ		*mouth*	mauþ
uncūð	uncuuþ		*uncouth*	əncuuþ
cūðe	cuu(l)d	1460	*could*	cud
būð N.	(buuþ)		*booth*	buuþ
ūs (*under* u)				
hūs	huus		*house*	haus
lūs	luus		*louse*	laus
þūsend	þuuzend	1464	*thousand*	þauzənd
mūs	muus		*mouse*	maus
scūfan (*under* u)				
dūfe (*under* u)				

h; r, hr, l, hl; ð, s, w, hw, f; ng, n, m; g, c, d, t, b, p.

ū (*continued*).

OLD.	MIDDLE.		MODERN.	
onbūfan (*under* u)				
scūnian (*under* u)				
dūn	duun		*down*	daun
tūn	tuun		*town*	taun
brūn	bruun	1468	*brown*	braun
þūma (*under* u)				
rūm	(ruum)		*room*	ruum
rūg	ruuh		*rough*	rəf
būgan	buu		*bow*	bau
sūcan (*under* u)				
brūcan	(bruuc)	1472	*brook*	bruc
ūder (*under* u)				
hlūd	luud		*loud*	laud
scrūd	shruud		*shroud*	shraud
crūd	cruud		*crowd*	craud
clūd	cluud	1476	*cloud*	claud
ūt	uut		*out*	aut
ūterlice (*under* u)				
lūtan	luut		*lout* (subst.)	laut
clūt	cluut		*clout*	claut
būtan (*under* u)				
prūt	pruud	1480	*proud*	praud
sūpan (*under* u)				

ó.

cohh(ett)an	còuh		*cough*	cof
sōhte	sòuht		*sought*	sòòt
wrohte	wròuht		*wrought*	ròòt
dohtor	dauhter	1484	*daughter*	dòòtər
bohte	bòuht		*bought*	bòòt
brohte	bròuht		*brought*	bròòt

a(æ ea ei), i, é(eo), è, ē, ǣ, eā, eō, u, o.

ó (*continued*).

OLD.	MIDDLE.		MODERN.	
for	for		*for*	fòòr
beforan	befòòr	1488	*before*	befòòr
borian	bòòr		*bore*	bòòr
woruld	wurld		*world*	wɔəld
forð	forþ		*forth*	fòɔþ
norð	norþ	1492	*north*	nòɔþ
morðor	murðer		*murder* (*th*)	məədər
hors	hors		*horse*	hòɔs
forst (*under* st)				
dorste	durst		*durst*	dɔəst
borsten	burst	1496	*burst*	bɔəst
horn	horn		*horn*	hòən
forlor(e)n	forlorn		*forlorn*	foəlòɔn
þorn	þorn		*thorn*	þòɔn
swor(e)n	sworn	1500	*sworn*	swòɔn
scor(e)n	shorn		*shorn*	shòɔn
mor(ge)ning	morning		*morning*	mòɔning
corn	corn		*corn*	còɔn
tor(e)n	torn	1504	*torn*	tòɔn
bor(e)n	born		*born*(*e*)	bòɔn
storm	storm		*storm*	stòəm
forma	former		*former*	fòəmər
sorg	soru	1508	*sorrow*	soróu
morgen	moru		*morrow*	moróu
borgian	boru		*borrow*	boróu
storc	storc		*stork*	stòəc
hord	hòòrd	1512	*hoard*	hòəd
word	word		*word*	wɔəd
ford	ford		*ford*	fòɔd
bord	bòòrd		*board*	bòɔd
scort	short	1516	*short*	shòət
port	port		*port*	pòət
hol	hòòl		*hole*	hóul
holh	holu		*hollow*	holou

h; r, hr, l, hl; ð, s, w, hw, f; ng, n, m; g, c, d, t, b, p.

ó (*continued*).

OLD.	MIDDLE.		MODERN.	
holegn	holi	1520	*holly*	holi
þol	þòòl		*thole(pin)*	þóul
swollen	swolen		*swollen*	swóuln
scolu	shòòl		*shoal*	shóul
stolen	stòòlen	1524	*stolen*	stóuln
fola	fòòl		*foal*	fóul
col	còòl		*coal*	cóul
cnoll	cnol		*knoll*	nóul
dol	dul	1528	*dull*	dəl
toll	tol		*toll*	tóul
bolla	bóul		*bowl*	bóul
bolster	bolster		*bolster*	bóulstər
folgian	folu	1532	*follow*	folou
wolcen	welcin		*welkin*	welcin
folc	folc		*folk*	fóuc
scolde	? shuuld		*should*	shud
molde	mould	1536	*mould*	móuld
wolde	? wuuld		*would*	wud
gold	gold		*gold*	góuld
bolt	bolt		*bolt*	bóult
froða N.	froþ	1540	*froth*	frò(ò)þ
moððe	moþ		*moth*	mò(ò)þ
broð	broþ		*broth*	bròòþ
hose	hòòz		*hose*	hóuz
*gefrosen	fròòzen	1544	*frozen*	fróuzn
nosu	nòòz		*nose*	nóuz
*gecosen	chòòzen		*chosen*	chóuzn
cross N.	cross		*cross*	cros
blōsma	blosom	1548	*blossom*	blosəm
gōsling	gosling		*gosling*	gozling
frost	frost		*frost*	frost
òf {	ov		*of*	ov
	of	1552	*off*	of
ofen	? òòven		*oven*	əvn

a(æ ea ei), i, é(eo), è, ē, ǣ, eā, eō, u, o.

ó (*continued*).

OLD.	MIDDLE.		MODERN.	
offrian	ofer		*offer*	ofər
ofer	òòver		*over*	óuvər
scofel	? shòòvel	1556	*shovel*	shəvl
clofen	clòòven		*cloven*	clóuvn
oft	oft		*oft*	oft
loft N.	loft		*loft*	loft
sōfte	soft	1560	*soft*	soft
lòng	long		*long*	long
þròng	þrong		*throng*	þrong
þwòng	þong		*thong*	þong
sòng *(subs.)*	song	1564	*song*	song
stròng	strong		*strong*	strong
wròng	wrong		*wrong*	rong
mòngere	monger (u)		*monger*	məngər
òngemòng	among (u)	1568	*among*	eməng
tònge	tongz		*tongs*	tongz
òn	on		*on*	on
bònd	bond		*bond*	bond
fròm	from	1572	*from*	from
wòmb	(wóómb)		*womb*	wuum
còmb	còòmb		*comb*	cóum
frocga	frog		*frog*	frog
trog	trouh	1576	*trough*	tròf
boga	bou		*bow*	bóu
flog(e)n	floun		*flown*	flóun
locc	loc		*lock*	loc
socc	soc	1580	*sock*	soc
smocc	smoc		*smock*	smoc
smoca	smòòc		*smoke*	smóuc
stocc	stoc		*stock*	stoc
*gesprocen	spòòcen	1584	*spoken*	spóucən
flocc	floc		*flock*	floc
geoc	yòòc		*yoke*	yóuc

ó (*continued*).

OLD.	MIDDLE.		MODERN.	
cocc	coc		*cock*	coc
coccel	cocl	1588	*cockle*	cocl
crocc	croc		*crock(ery)*	croc(əri)
cnocian	cnoc		*knock*	noc
brocen	bròòcen		*broken*	bróucən
oxa	ox	1592	*ox*	ox
fox	fox		*fox*	fox
rōd	rod		*rod*	rod
soden	soden		*sodden*	sodn
gescōd	shod	1596	*shod*	shod
fōdor	foder		*fodder*	fodər
god	god		*god*	god
codd	cod		*cod*	cod
troden	troden	1600	*trodden*	trodn
bodian	bòòd		*bode*	bóud
bodig	bodi		*body*	bodi
rotian	rot		*rot*	rot
hlot	lot	1604	*lot*	lot
þrotu	þròòt		*throat*	þróut
(ge)scot	shot		*shot*	shot
scotland	scotland		*Scotland*	scotlənd
flotian	flòòt	1608	*float*	flóut
mot	mòòt		*mote*	móut
cot	cot		*cot*	cot
cnotta	cnot		*knot*	not
botm	botom	1612	*bottom*	botəm
loppestre	lobster		*lobster*	lobstər
open	òòpen		*open*	óupən
hoppian	hop		*hop*	hop
hopa	hòòp	1616	*hope*	hóup
sop	sop		*sop*	sop
stoppian	stop		*stop*	stop
(āttor)coppa	cob(web)		*cob(web)*	cob(web)
cropp	crop	1620	*crop*	crop
dropa	drop		*drop*	drop
topp	top		*top*	top

a(æ ea ei), i, é(eo), è, ē, ǣ, eā, eō, u, o.

ō.

OLD.	MIDDLE.			MODERN.
scō	(shóó)		*shoe*	shuu
dō	(dóó)	1624	*do*	duu
tō	tóó		*too, to*	tuu
tōh	tuuh		*tough*	təf
? sōhte, etc. (*under* o)				
hōr	(w)hòòr		*whore*	hòòr
swōr	swòòr	1628	*swore*	swòòr
flōr	flóór		*floor*	flòòr
mōr	móór		*moor*	muər
stōl	stóól		*stool*	stuul
cōl	cóól	1632	*cool*	cuul
tōl	tóól		*tool*	tuul
ōðer	(óóðer)		*other*	əðər
sōð	sóóþ		*sooth*	suuþ
*smōðe	smóóð	1636	*smooth*	smuuð
*(hē) dōð	dóóþ		*doth*	dəþ
tōð	tóóþ		*tooth*	tuuþ
brōðor	(bróóðer)		*brother*	brəðər
gōs	góós	1640	*goose*	guus
gōsling (*under* o)				
bōsm	(bóózəm)		*bosom*	buzəm
blōsma (*under* o)				
hrōst	róóst		*roost*	ruust
mōste	must		*must*	məst
rōwan	róu	1644	*row*	róu
hlōwan	lóu		*low*	lóu
flōwan	flóu		*flow*	flóu
grōwan	gróu		*grow*	gróu
blōwan	blóu	1648	*blow*	blóu
hōf *(pret.)*	(hóóv)		*hove*	hóuv
hōf *(subs.)*	hóóf		*hoof*	huuf
behōfian	(behóóv)		*behove*	behuuv (óu)
grōf *(subs.)*	gróóv	1652	*groove*	gruuv
glōf	(glóóv)		*glove*	gləv

h; r, hr, l, hl; ð, s, w, hw, f; ng, n, m; g, c, d, t, b, p.

ō (*continued*).

OLD.	MIDDLE.		MODERN.	
sōfte (*under* o)				
sōna	sóón		*soon*	suun
spōn N. ?	spóón		*spoon*	spuun
nōn	nóón	1656	*noon*	nuun
mōna	móón		*moon*	muun
mōnað	(móóneþ)		*moneth*, *month*	mənþ
mōnandæg	(móóndai)		*Monday*	məndi
gedōn	(dóón)	1660	*done*	dən
bōn N.	bóón		*boon*	buun
gōma	gum		*gum*	gəm
glōm	glóóm		*gloom*	gluum
dōm	dóóm	1664	*doom*	duum
brōm	bróóm		*broom*	bruum
blōma	blóóm		*bloom*	bluum
slōg	sleu		*slew*	sluu
wōgian	wóó	1668	*woo*	wuu
genōg	enuuh		*enough*	enəf
drōg	dreu		*drew*	druu
bōg	buuh		*bough*	bau
plōg N.	pluuh	1672	*plough*	plau
hōc	hóóc		*hook*	huc
hrōc	róóc		*rook*	ruc
lōcian	lóóc		*look*	luc
scōc	shóóc	1676	*shook*	shuc
wōc	(awóóc)		*awoke*	əwóuc
cōc	cóóc		*cook*	cuc
crōc N.	cróóc		*crook*	cruc
tōc	tóóc	1680	*took*	tuc
bōc	bóóc		*book*	buc
brōc	bróóc		*brook*	bruc
hōd	hóód		*hood*	hud
rōd {	róód	1684	*rood*	ruud
	rod		*rod*	rod
gescōd (*under* o)				
stōd	stóód		*stood*	stud
fōda	fóód		*food*	fuud
fōdor (*under* o)				
flōd	flóód	1688	*flood*	fləd
mōd	móód		*mood*	muud

a(æ ea ei), i, é(eo), è, ē, ǣ, eā, eō, u, o.

ō (*continued*).

OLD.	MIDDLE.		MODERN.	
mōdor	(móóðer)		*mother*	məðər
gōd	góód		*good*	gud
blōd	blóód	1692	*blood*	bləd
brōd	bróód		*brood*	bruud
wōdnesdæg	wednesdai		*Wednesday*	we(d)nzdi
rōt N.	róót		*root*	ruut
fōt	fóót	1696	*foot*	fut
bōt	bóót		*boot*	buut
hwōpan	whóóp		*whoop*	huup

Addenda.

mearg	maru		*marrow*	mærou
cealc	chalc	1700	*chalk*	chòòc
hæsel	haazel		*hazel*	héizl
sceanc	shanc		*shank*	shænc
wæg(e)n	wagon		*waggon*	wægən
	wain	1704	*wain*	wéin
dragen	draun		*drawn*	dròòn
? gagn	gain		*gain*	géin
sæcc	sac		*sack*	sæc
sleac	slac	1708	*slack*	slæc
wæcce	wach		*watch*	woch
gemaca	maat		*mate*	méit
eaxl	axl		*axle*	æxl
lator	later	1712	*latter*	lætər
gabb N.	gab		*gab*	gæb
tapor	taaper		*taper*	téipər
ār (*metal*)	òòr		*ore*	òòr
hālig dæg	? hòòlidaj	1716	*holiday*	holidi
rāw	ròòu		*row*	róu
*cnāwlǣcan	cnòòulej		*knowledge*(sbst.)	nolej
òn ān	anon		*anon*	ənon

h; r, hr, l, hl; ð, s, w, hw, f; ng, n, m; g, c, d, t, b, p.

ADDENDA (*continued*).

OLD.	MIDDLE.		MODERN.	
wrist	wrist	1720	*wrist*	rist
hiw	heu		*hue (hew)*	hyuu
skipta N.	shift		*shift*	shift
wringan	wring		*wring*	ring
slipor	sliperi	1724	*slippery*	sliperi
hwīnan	whiin		*whine*	whain
cyrnel	cernel		*kernel*	cəənəl
sȳpan	sip		*sip*	sip
féðer	fèèðer	1728	*feather*	feðər
becwéðan	becwèèð		*bequeathe*	becwiið
wést	west		*west*	west
weocce	wic		*wick*	wic
rǣdels	ridl	1732	*riddle*	ridl
gemēted	met		*met*	met
stèrne	stern		*stern*	stəən
rest	rest		*rest*	rəst
wrèncan	wrench	1736	*wrench*	rench
wrǣnna	wren		*wren*	ren
twèntig	twenti		*twenti*	twenti
hēhðo	heiht		*height*	hait
stēran	stéér	1740	*steer*	stiər
cwēn	cwèèn		*quean* [1]	cwiin
? leās	lóós		*loose*	luus
þreātian	þrèèt		*threat*	þret
preōst	(préést)	1744	*priest*	priist
seōc	sic		*sick*	sic
þohte	þòuht		*thought*	þòòt
colt	colt		*colt*	cóult
fōstor	foster	1748	*foster*	fostər
hrōf	róóf		*roof*	ruuf
þus	ðus		*thus*	ðəs
húsþing N.	hustingz		*hustings*	həstingz
suncen	sunc	1752	*sunk*	sənc
skūm	scum		*skum*	scəm

a(æ ea ei), i, é(eo), è, ē, ǣ, eā, eō, u, o.

[1] Seems to come from *cwéne* with a short vowel = Gothic *kwinō*.

ALPHABETICAL INDEX TO THE LISTS.[1]

[1] Numbers in parentheses refer to words in the Addenda.

SUPPLEMENTARY LISTS OF IRREGULARITIES.

Middle Period.

In the following words *æ* and *ea* have become *e* instead of the regular *a*: *gèèr* (gear), *èèrn* (earn), *fern*, *bèèrd* (beard); *elf*, *belch*; *wheðer*, *togeðer*; *les*, *nes*, *lest*, *lèèst* (least), *gest* (guest); *ðen*, *when*; *emet*, *hemp*; *wrec*, *pebl*.

It is clear from these exceptional forms that the Old English *æ* was quite lost after the Transition period; as we see, it was either changed into *a*, or else mispronounced as *è*, just as it would be in the mouth of a foreigner.

The lengthening before *r* in *gèèr*, *èèrn* and *bèèrd* has many parallels, and in the case of *bèèrd* is confirmed by the Modern *biiəd*. The present form *əən*, however, points rather to *ern*, with a short vowel. The lengthening in *lèèst*, although anomalous, is supported by *yèèst* from *yest*=*gist*, by the retention of *òò*=*ā* in *mòòst*, etc., and perhaps by *criist* (see note on 518, below).

a for *ò* in non-preterites (p. 54): *angl*, *hang*, *fang*, *gang*, *bang*.

ò for *a*: *on*, *bond*, *from*, *womb*, *comb*.

ei preserved: *ei* (eye), *ðei* (they), *whei, grei, cei* (key); *weih* (weigh), *neih, neih(buur), eiht* (eight), *heiht; ðeir; eiðer; rein(déér)*.

The Modern forms point mostly to *ai*. *ai* (eye) however comes not from *ai=ei*, but from *ii*. *cii* (key) is altogether anomalous; so also are the two pronunciations *iiðer* and *aiðər* (either), while the obsolete *éiðər* is regular.

i (*y*) has become *e*, 1) regularly after *y*-consonant: *yel; yes, yèèst, yesterdai; yet.* 2) in other words: *her, herd* (shep-(herd); *neðer; ðèèz* (these); *èèvil; flejd* (fledged).

In *snèèc* and *rèèp* (sneak, reap) a highly anomalous change of *ii* into *èè* seems to have taken place.

é, eo become *i*: *liht, fiht*; *mirþ* (but *meri*), *birch; chil, silver, silc, milc, fiild; sister; ric, wic; cripl, hip* (=berry), *dip* (?).

è becomes *i*: *smirc, gird(l); sili, cil, wiild; linc; rid; nib.*

é becomes *a*, 1) before *r*: *star, far, tar, darling* (from *deōrling*), *farðing, carv, starv, barm, dwarf, baru, darc, harc, hart.* 2) in: *swalu, brambl.*

è becomes *a*, 1) before *r*: *mar, maar, barlei, marsh, haru, barn, yard.* 2) in: *talu* (?); *wasp; handi* (?), *aach.*

é, eo become *u*: *churl, burst, run, spurn, burn; hung.*

ē, eō become *ii*: *ii* (from *eāge*), *lii* (from *leōgan*), *slii, flii, tii; hiih, þiih, niih; diiv* (?).

ē becomes *èè* before *r*: *hèèr, wèèri, hèèren, hèèrd.*

In the case of the first two words there is sixteenth century authority for the *éé*-sound also.

ǣ=éé becomes *èè*, 1) before *r* in all words except the doubtful *béér*. 2) in: *mèèl; brèèð; èèven* (evening); *þrèèd, drèèd; blèèt; wèèpon.*

Three of these, however, are made doubtful by the Modern *þred, dred, wepon*, which point rather to a shortening of the long vowel at an early period.

eō becomes *èè*: *dèèr, drèèri; brèèst, clèèv* (cleave).

There is Early Modern authority for *déér* as well as *dèèr*. *brèèst*, again, is uncertain on account of the Modern *brest.*

eō becomes *óó*: *lóóz, chóóz; shóót.*

Compare *chòòz* from *ceās* (p. 35), and *ðòòuh* from *þeāh* (note to 1228, below).

eō becomes *u*(*u*): *yuu; ruuh; yuuþ; yung.*[1]

o becomes *u*: *murðer, durst, burst* (partic.); *dul; amung, munger.*

ō becomes *u*(*u*): *yuu* (you); *tuuh* (tough); *yuuþ*; *yung.*

The following remarks on the diphthongs are intended to supplement those on pp. 52, 53, above.

Diphthongs are formed not only by *g* (*gh*), but also by medial and final *h* (=*kh*), but only with back vowels, the new element being always *u* (never *i*), which I have already explained (note p. 80) as a mere *secondary* formation, due to the labialization of the following *h*=*kh*: the *h* is consequently not absorbed, as is the case with *g*.

The following are examples of genuine *h*-diphthongs, in which *h* is original, not a later modification of *g* (p. 79):

1) from *ah*: *lauh, lauhter, slauhter, fauht, tauht.* And perhaps *sau* from *seah*, although the omission of the *h* makes it more probable that it arises from some confusion with the plural *sāwon.*
2) from *āh*: *òòuht* (ought).
   not points to *nòòuht*=*nāht*; *nauht*, however, to a shortened *naht*.
3) from *oh*: *souht, bouht, bouht.*
   For *dauhter* see note to 1484.

In the following words *g* has been anomalously preserved, instead of being diphthongized: *wag, wagon* (but also *wain*), *drag* (but also *drau*), *twig*.

A few general remarks on Middle (or rather Early Modern) English orthography remain to be made.

It is, as we have seen, mainly traditional, but with certain purely phonetic modifications. The first divergence of sound and symbol was the retention of *ee* and *oo* to denote the new sounds *ii* and *uu*, while original *ii* and *uu* themselves changed in the direction of *ai* and *au*. The introduction of *ea* and *oa* to denote the true *ee* and *oo* sound was, on the other hand, a strictly phonetic innovation.

ee and *oo* were partly phonetic, partly historical signs—

[1] I have repeated most of these words again under *ō*.

they denoted the sounds *ii* and *uu*, and implied at the same time an earlier *éé* and *óó*. But in a few cases it is interesting to observe that they were employed purely phonetically, *against* tradition. An example is afforded by the word written *room*, the Old English *rūm*. In the fourteenth century this word was spelt with the French *ou*=*uu*; but in the Early Modern period the regular *rowm*, corresponding with *down*, etc., was abandoned, probably because it would, like *down*, have suggested the regular diphthong *óu* or *ɔu*, into which the other old *uu*s changed, and the word was written phonetically *room*, without at all implying a Middle English *róóm*. Other examples are *door* and *groom*, in which *oo* may perhaps represent short *u*, which it almost certainly does in *wool* and *wood*. The use of single *o* to denote short *u* is a well-known feature of Middle English. It occurs chiefly in combination with *w*, *u*(=*v*), *n*, and *m*, and has been explained (first, I believe, by Dr. J. A. H. Murray) as a purely graphic substitute for *u* in combination with letters of similar formation, to avoid confusion. But such a spelling as *wod* would have suggested an *ò*-sound, as in *god*. To avoid all possibility of this pronunciation, the *o* was therefore doubled. This spelling is only inaccurate as regards the quantity; it is, therefore, difficult to see why it was not adopted in the words written *love*, *come*, etc., which ought by their spelling to indicate the pronunciations *lóóv*, *cóóm*, corresponding to Middle English *lòòv*, *còòm*!

Similar fluctuation between the phonetic and historical principle is shown in many words written with the digraph *ie*. *ie* is in itself nothing but a substitute for *ii*, which from purely graphic reasons was never doubled, as being liable to confusion with *u*. The sound of *ii* was, of course, in most cases expressed by *ee*. There were, however, a few words which preserved their Middle English *ii*-sound throughout the Early Modern period (and up to the present day) as well. Such a word as *fiild*, for instance, if written in the fourteenth century spelling *fild*, would have been read, on the analogy of *wild*, *child*, etc., as *féild*, or *fɔild*, while to have written *feeld* would have been a violation of the etymological principle. Both history and sound were saved by the adoption of *ie*. The following list of *ie*-words will show that, although *ie* was sometimes used finally to denote the diphthongized sound, it invariably denoted the simple *ii* medially: *hie, lie, die, tie; wierd; yield, shield, wield, field; priest; believe, sieve; lief, thief; fiend, friend.*

In *sieve* we have an instance of *ie* used to denote a short vowel (compare *wool*, etc.); possibly the *ie* was employed simply to prevent the combination *siue*, which would have been graphically ambiguous.

Modern Period.

The general rule which governs the retention and modification of *a* before sibilants seems to be that it is retained before breath consonants, but changed to *æ* before voice consonants. Thus we find *æz, hæz, hæv* contrasting with *a(a)s, gras, asc, last, staf, after.* The change to *æ* takes place, however, before *sh*, although voiceless: *æsh, ræsh.* Also in *æspen.*[1] In the same way *a* followed by *n* and a voice consonant becomes *æ*, as in *ænd, hænd, ænvil*; but if the consonant which comes after the *n* is voiceless, there is no change, as in *ansər, plant, ant.* These laws do not apply to *a* when followed by the other nasals, in which cases it is always changed: *sænc, drænc; dæmp.*

ii has been preserved in the following words: *mii: shiiər, wiiəd; shiild, wiild, fiild, yiild; wiivəl, wiic.*

Of these words the first only has *ī* in O.E.; all the others are Middle E. lengthenings of *i*, corresponding sometimes to original *i*, sometimes to *è* or *é*. It is worthy of note that all of them are written with *ie*, except *shiiər, wiivəl*, and *wiik*, which are written *shire, weevil, week.* The last two spellings with *e*, which go back as far as the fourteenth century, seem to indicate some confusion with *éé*, although we would rather expect the broad *èè*, as in *snèèc* for *sniic*. It is, however,

[1] Note, however, that *aspen* is a dissyllable, with a liquid in the second syllable: but we have *after*, not *æfter.*

possible that these *ee*s may be simply Early Modern phonetic spellings, like *room*=*ruum*.

èè has become *éi* (instead of *ii*) : *yéi* (yea) ; *bréic* ; *gréit*.[1]

u has been preserved, 1) after *w* : *wuman*, *wul*, *wulf*, *wuund*, *wud* (not in *wəndər*). 2) in other cases : *ful*, *bul(əc)* ; *grum*.

uu has been preserved (sometimes with shortening) : *buur* (boor) ; *əncuuþ* ; *cud* (could) ; *ruum* (room) ; *bruc* (brook).

óó has been preserved : *hóuv* ; *əwóuc*.

óó has become *ə* : *əðer*, *məðer*, *dəþ*, *brəðər* ; *gləv* ; *mənþ*, *məndi*, *dən* ; *fləd*, *bləd*.

For *əvn* and *shəvl* see notes to 1553 and 1556.

The series of changes is clearly *óó*, *uu*, *u*, *ə* ; the second and third belonging to the Early Modern, the last to the Transition period. The anomalous spelling *other*, etc., instead of *oother*, was probably meant to indicate the shortness of the *u*=*óó*. To infer from it a Middle E. *òòðer* would be as unreasonable as in the case of *love*, *come*, etc., where the *u* was certainly never lengthened or lowered to *òò*.

Under the head of consonant influence the loss of the initial element of the diphthong *iuu* or *yuu* ought to have been noticed in its place. It takes place after *r* and *l*, but not after stops, nasals, and sibilants : *ruu*, *gruu*, *cruu* ; *fluu*, *cluu*; also in *chuu* (*lyuud* is an exception), *yuu*; *hyuu*; *þyuu*; *fyuu* ; *nyuu* ; *dyuu* ; *styuu* ; *spyuu*.

The development of the diphthong *óu* out of *ol* in the combination *olc* ought also to have been noticed ; it occurs in two words : *yóuc* (yolk), *fóuc* (folk).

Also the change of *a* into *ò* before *lt*, in *holt*, *solt*, *molt*.

NOTES TO THE WORD LISTS.

No. 3. *eiht*. A solitary exception to the general change of *aht* into *auht*. There is Early Mod. evidence for *aiht* as well as *eiht*.

[1] For the preservation of *èè* before *r* in *bèèr*, etc., see p. 68.

6. *fauht.* Salesbury writes *fauht*, and the spelling *fought* seems merely due to confusion with the partic. *fouhten* from O.E. *gefohten*.

15. *năru*, etc. These words are not derived direct from the nom. *nearu*, but from the oblique cases, *nearwe* becoming *nearw*, whence *naru*, by weakening of the final *w*. *caru*, on the other hand, which has *care* in the oblique cases, naturally lengthens its vowel—*caar*.

25. *gèèr* from *gearwa* is only an apparent exception to the rule just stated, the long vowel being probably due to the *r*. The loss of the *w* is, however, anomalous.

58. *shæl*, for *shòòl*. An isolated exception to the development of *au* before *l*.

68. *ceallian.* This word occurs in the poem of Byrhtnoð; it may therefore possibly be English, although Norse influence in so late a work is quite possible.

71. *baal.* Exceptionally taken from the nom. *bealu*, not from the oblique *bealw-* (see note to 15, above).

81. *psalm.* The *p* is, of course, purely pedantic; the word may, however, be French.

84. *tælg.* The vowel is doubtful, and I have given the word again under *è* (992).

89, 91. *alder, alderman.* The exceptional retention of the *a* may be due to the liquid in the second syllable: compare the short *i* in *wunder*, etc., as contrasted with *wuund* (p. 47).

132. *castel.* This word, although of French origin, was in familiar use in English many years before the Conquest.

140. *hauc*, from *havoc* through *havec*, *haw(e)c*. The converse change has taken place in *waav* (1170); the series was probably *wǣg*, *waaw*, *waav*.

150. *clòòver.* The only parallel is *lòòd* from *hladan* (298).

168, 169. *monger, among.* The *u*-sound, for which there is Early Middle authority, as well as for *o*, is anomalous.

181. *eni.* The Early form (or one of them) was *ani* with short *a* (as Gill expressly states); the present form *eni* may therefore be explained as an irregular variation of the normal *æni*.

182. *hemp* seems to point to an O.E. *hænep* (cp. 187).

187, 193. *then, when.* These clearly arise from the Late O.E. *ðænne* and *whænne* with abnormal modification of *a* before nasals (p. 26).

229. *swæm* for *swòm*. *m* seems to bar the retention of *a* for *æ* in the same way in the word *dæmp* (p. 150).

246, 248. *slai, flai,* instead of *slau, flau.* The subs. *slège* may have helped the former irregularity.

253. *daun.* *dag(e)nian* ought to give *dain,* but the analogy of the regular Middle E. *dawes* from *dagas* helped.

270. *acorn.* The *o* is probably inorganic, the result of association with *corn.*

298. *lòòd.* cp. *clòòver* (150).

303. *shaad* for *sceadw-.* cp. *baal,* 71.

324. *water.* The Modern *wòòter,* with its long vowel, is anomalous.

331. *got,* inorganic, from the analogy of the partic. **begoten.*

343. *pebl,* from *pæpol* or *pæbol* (?).

344. *ai.* The modern form is a solitary case of retention of the diphthong.

350. *rein.* The older spelling *raindeer* should have been given.

352. The Middle *stèèc* and its change into the Modern *stéic* are both anomalous.

353. *weak* may possibly come from the O.E. *wāc,* through *wǣc.*

355. *dii,* from *dey(ja)* ; cp. *ii* for *ei* from *cāge* (1121).

357. *lā.* If the Modern *lòò* (written *law*) really corresponds to the O.E. *lā,* we have a second instance (besides *bròòd*) of the retention of *òò.* *treysta* (770) should have been referred to here.

372. *haal.* A solitary and dubious instance of the retention of O.E. *ā.*

389. *nothing.* The Modern *ə* is probably due to the analogy of *wən* (415) and *nən.*

396. *whòòz,* read *whóóz.* The Modern *uu* is better evidence than the spelling *whose.*

400. *þau,* points seemingly to an O.E. *þăwan.*

415. *wən.* The most probable explanation is that *wə* is

simply the Early Modern *óó* with its labial and guttural elements pronounced successively instead of simultaneously (p. 14).

418. *nən*. Not a case of *òò* becoming *ə* through *uu* and *u*, but simply due to the analogy of *wən*.

429. *clami*. The O.E. *ā* in this word must have been shortened at a very early period, else we should have had *clomi*.

440. *-hóód*. A solitary instance of *òò* becoming *óó* in Middle English (except after *w*).

447. *bròòd*. Retention of Middle English *òò* from *ā*.

491. *gild*. Exceptional retention of short *i*. cp. *gild* (from *gyldan*) and *byld* (760, 761).

518. *criist*. The *ch* is, of course, no evidence; but the word may be French. Compare, however, *lèèst* (126) and *yèèst* (520), with the same lengthening before *st*.

528. *teuzdai*. The spelling *ue* indicates the later simplification *yy*.

534. *wiivil*. It is uncertain whether the spelling *ee* indicates a Middle English *wéévil* or is purely phonetic.

604. *island*. The *s* is purely etymological and erroneous.

707. *rich*. May be French.

760, 761. *gild, byld*. Exceptional retention of the short vowels. There is, however, Early Middle authority for *byyld* as well.

796. *luck*. The word *lukka* in Icelandic is said to be of late introduction, otherwise it would fit in very well. I have formed *lycci* from the Danish *lykke*.

847. *þræsh* may be a modification of *þresh*, as *eni* seems to be of *æni* (181).

860. *iceberg*. Probably foreign (Dutch?).

868. *swurd*; or from *u* (1365).

870. *hèèrt* and *hart* are both independent modifications of *hèrt*.

881. *cwail*. Compare *hair* (1157) from *hǣr*. The history of these two spellings requires investigation: it is possible that the *ai* is merely a comparatively late representation of the sound *èè*, introduced after the simplification of the diphthong *ai* (p. 65).

934. *þaan* for *þain*. Here, again, the spelling may be late. The Modern *þéin* would correspond to either *þaan* or *þain*.

956. *nebb*. The vowel is more probably *è* (1087).

1005. *wasp* points rather to *wæsp* than *wèsp*; both forms may, however, have existed.

1017. *wǣng* (551) should come in here.

1036. *clenz*. The spelling *ea* certainly points to *clèènz*, but the Modern form is against it, and it is possible that the *ea* may be a purely etymological reminiscence.

1038. *handi* may be merely a late derivative of *hand*.

1052. *temz*. The spelling is evidently a pedantic adaptation of the Latin *T(h)amesis*.

1054. *au*. This form (instead of *ai*) is very anomalous. The most probable explanation is that *ège* was made into *æge* by the same confusion between the two vowels as in *wèsp* (1005), and that *æge* then became *age*, which was irregularly diphthongized into *au(e)*.

1057. *hej* points rather to *hècg* than *hège*, which would give *hai*.

1058, 1060. *lai*, *sai*. These forms (instead of *lej*, *sej*) point rather to some such inflection as the imperative *lège*, *sège*.

1064. *aach*. Another case of confusion between *è* and *æ*—*ècc*, *æcc*, *acc*, *aach*.

1105. *cnēla*. The Icelandic expression is *knéfalla*, but *knæle* is found in Danish.

1135. *read*. I have given the word again under *èè* (1218), as it is quite uncertain whether it had *ē* or *ǣ* in O.E.: the assumed derivation from *rōdjan* favours the former, the MSS. usage the latter.

1157. *hair*. cp. *cwail* (881).

1171. *weih*, etc. Anomalous retention of *gh* in the form of *h*.

1228. *ðòòuh*. The stages were probably *ðeaah*, *ðaah*, *ðòòh*, *ðòòuh*.

1239. *rau*. Apparently from an intermediate *hreāw*; cp. *þau* (400).

1241, 1242. *slòòu, shòòu.* The same dropping of the first element of O.E. *eaa*, as in the previous word. All these forms are important, as showing that the second element of the diphthong had the accent and was long.

1244. *strau.* cp. 1239.

1276. *chapman.* Points to a shortened *ea*, which naturally passed into *a*.

1292. *darling.* From shortened *eo* — *deōr-, deor-, der-, dar-ling.*

1295. *fourþ.* Probably formed directly from the Middle English *four* itself.

1306. *yuu.* Here the first element of the diphthong is consonantized, and the final *w* thrown off, as in *tréé, cnéé*, etc.

1333. *friend.* The Modern *frend* points to a very early shortened form, which probably co-existed with the older *fréénd.*

1353, 1363. *thorough, borough.* The Modern *ə* points to *þuruh* and *buruh*, and it is possible that the *o* is a mere graphic substitute for *u*.

1370. *shóulder* for *shaulder.* The most probable explanation is that *shuulder* became *shóulder* in the Early Modern period, and the *óu* became *óóu* before *ld*, and so was confounded with the *óóu* in *flóóu*, etc.

1380. *eleven.* Agrees rather with the other form *endleofon.*

1460. *cuuld.* The *l* is, of course, due to the analogy of *wuuld* and *shuuld.*

1470. *ruuh* may possibly come from *hreōh* (1288).

1484. *dauhter.* The anomalous *au* may be due to Norse influence, as Danish has *datter* (Icelandic *dóttir*): I do not know, however, that the Danish form is of any antiquity.

1519. *holu.* The final *h* of *holh* seems to have been first vocalized (and labialized), and then merged into *w*, which, as in *naru*, etc., was weakened into *u*.

1521. *swóuln*, etc. The development of *ou* in the combinations *ol, old*, is Early Modern, and should have been mentioned (p. 61). The phoneticians make the *o* long, writing *tooul* (=*toll*), etc. Its preservation in the present English is, therefore, quite regular, as in *flóu* from Middle E. *flóóu*, etc.

1530. *bóul.* Here, again, the sixteenth century authorities write *booul.* The spelling *bowl* is, of course, phonetic and unhistorical.

1533. *welcin.* cp. *wednesdai* (1694).

1540. *froþ*, etc. The quantity of *o* before *þ*, *s*, and *f* is very uncertain in the present English, but the longs seem to be getting the upper hand.

1553. *oven.* The Modern *əvn* points rather to *óóven* than the regular *òòven.*

1556. *shovel.* The Modern *shəvl*, again, points to an earlier *shuvl*, which may be a shortening of *shuuvel*=*shóóvel*, as was suggested in the case of *oven.* Or the form *shuvel* may be due to the analogy of the verb *shuv*=*scūfan.*

1667, 1670. *sleu*, *dreu.* The most probable explanation is that *slóóg* first became *slóóu*, and then this was confused with the numerous preterites in *eóów* (*greōw*, *cneōw*, etc.), and followed the same change into *eu.*

1694. *wednesday.* cp. *welcin* (1533).

ON THE PERIODS OF ENGLISH.

One of the most troublesome questions of English philology is that of the designation of its various stages. I have throughout this paper adopted the threefold division of Old, Middle, and Modern: it will, therefore, be necessary to say a few words in its justification.

The first question is, shall we retain the name "Anglo-Saxon" for the earliest period of our language, or discard it entirely? The great majority of English scholars are decidedly hostile to the word. They argue that it is a barbarous half-Latin compound, which, although justifiable as applied to a political confederation of Angles and Saxons, is entirely misleading when applied to the *language* spoken by these tribes, implying, as it does, that the English language before the Conquest was an actual mixture of the Anglian and Saxon dialects. The reverse was of course the case, and we consequently have to distinguish between the Anglian dialect of Anglo-Saxon and the Saxon dialect of Anglo-Saxon.[1] The most serious objection, however, to the word Anglo-Saxon is that it conceals the unbroken development of our language, and thrusts the oldest period of our language outside the pale of our sympathies. Hence, to a great extent, the slowness with which the study of our language makes its way among the great mass of educated people in England—if people can be called educated who are ignorant of the history of their own language.

These arguments have lately been vigorously attacked by a leading English philologist—Professor March. In his able essay[2] he brings out the distinctive features of the two extreme periods very forcibly, and has so far done good service. At the same time, he has greatly exaggerated the difference between the two periods. Thus, in phonology, he says that Anglo-Saxon had sounds now lost in English, such as French *u*, German *ch*, and initial *wl*, *wr*, and that *ī* and *ū* have become diphthongs. Now any one who has read this paper with any attention will see that this part of the argument is worth very little, for all these sounds were preserved unchanged in the sixteenth century, which belongs unmistakably to the Modern period.

The well-known statement that Johnson's Dictionary contains 29,000 Romance words out of 43,500 is a great exaggeration. A large proportion of these 29,000 are words which are never used in ordinary speech or writing, very many of them are quite unknown to the majority of educated people, and not a few of them never existed in the language at all. When we speak of the proportion of Romance elements in English, we mean the English of every-day life, not of dictionaries and technical works,[3] and of the two ex-

[1] If any period of our language is to be called "Anglo-Saxon," let it be the present one—as far, at least, as the literary language is concerned, which is really a mixture of Saxon and Anglian forms.

[2] Is there an Anglo-Saxon Language? Transactions of the American Philological Association, 1872.

[3] On such one-sided grounds as these it would be easy to prove that Modern German is quite as mixed as English is. Observe the proportion of foreign and native words in the following passages, taken at random from a work published this year:

"Wieniawski, der Paganinispieler *par excellence*, zeigt sich da, wo er mit

tremes, the estimate of Turner is certainly fairer than that of Thommerel.

The real distinction between the two stages lies, of course, in the comparatively uninflectional character of the present language and its analytical reconstruction. But the old inflections are not all lost; we still have our genitive, our plurals in *s* and *en*, and in our verbs the Teutonic strong preterite is still common. And it must be borne in mind that even the Oldest English inflections are beginning to break up. There is no *s* or *r* in the nominative singular, consequently no distinction between nominative and accusative in many words, no distinction whatever of gender in the plural of adjectives, or of person in the plural of verbs. The imperfect case terminations are already eked out by prepositions—*hē cwæð tō mē* is much more like English than Latin or even German.

And if we take the intermediate stages into consideration, we find it simply impossible to draw a definite line. Professor March acknowledges this, but takes refuge in a distinction between colloquial and literary speech, which last, he says, has much more definite periods. Professor March surely forgets that for scientific purposes artificial literary speech is worth nothing compared with that of every-day life, with its unconscious, unsophisticated development. It is, besides, very questionable whether there ever was an artificial literary prose language in England in early times.

While differing from Professor March on these points, I fully agree with him in protesting against the loose way in which "Old English" is made to designate any period from Alfred to Chaucer. It is quite clear that the inflectional stage of our language must have a distinctive name, and therefore that Old English must be reserved for it alone.

Schwierigkeiten und *Effecten à la* Paganini spielt, in seinem eigentlichen *Elemente;* seine *Compositionen* sind daher für *exclusive Virtuosen* nicht ohne *Interesse.* Dieselben wollen mit vollkommenster *technischer* Freiheit, übermüthiger Laune und Feuer gespielt sein, vor allen die *Variationen Opus* 11—echte *musikalische Mixpickles.*"

"Ein *effect*volles *Virtuosen*stück in Paganini'scher *Manier.*"

"Das kurze *Thema* ist mit *poetischer Simplicität* zu spielen."

Compare these specimens with the Lord's Prayer, or a page of Swift or Defoe.

The difficulty is with the later stages. The period I call Middle English is now often called "Early English," while those who retain "Anglo-Saxon" call the intermediate periods "Semi-Saxon" or "Old English," while others make various arbitrary distinctions between "Early," "Old," and "Middle" English. It does not seem to be generally acknowledged that each of these terms really implies a definite correlative, that if we call one period "Early," we are bound to have a "Late" one, and that "Middle" implies a beginning and an end—to talk therefore of one period as "Early," as opposed to a "Middle" one, is entirely arbitrary.

Such divisions err also in being too minute. When we consider how one period merges into another, and how the language changed with much greater rapidity in the North than in the South, we see that it is necessary to start with a few broad divisions, not with impracticably minute ones.

I propose, therefore, to start with the three main divisions of *Old*, *Middle*, and *Modern*, based mainly on the inflectional characteristics of each stage. Old English is the period of *full* inflections (*nama, gifan, caru*), Middle English of *levelled* inflections (*naame, given, caare*), and Modern English of *lost* inflections (*naam, giv, caar*). We have besides two periods of *transition*, one in which *nama* and *name* exist side by side, and another in which final *e* is beginning to drop. The latter is of very little importance, the former, commonly called Semi-Saxon (a legitimate abbreviation of Semi-Anglo-Saxon), is characterized by many far-reaching changes. I propose, therefore to call the first the *Transition* period *par excellence*, distinguishing the two, when necessary, as first and second Transition, the more important one being generally called simply *Transition* or *Transition-English*.

Whenever minute divisions are wanted, *Early* and *Late* can be used—Early Old, Late Middle, Early Modern, etc. Still minuter distinctions can be made by employing *Earlier*, *Earliest*, etc., till we fall back on the century or decade.

These divisions could also be applied to the different dialect-names. Thus *Old Anglian* would be equivalent to "Anglian dialect of Old English," *Modern Saxon* would designate the Dorsetshire dialect, etc.

As regards the Northern dialects of the Middle period, they ought strictly to be classed as Modern, as they soon lost the final *e* entirely. But as they have all the other characteristics of the Middle period, it seems most convenient to take the dominant speech of Chaucer and Gower as our criterion.

CONCLUDING REMARKS.

First of all I have a few words to say on the relation of the present essay to Mr. Ellis's great work.

As regards my obligations to Mr. Ellis, I can only say, once for all, that without his investigations this essay would never have been written. It is essentially based on his results, of which, in some places, it is little more than a summary; while I have throughout drawn largely on the enormous mass of material stored up in the "Early English Pronunciation."

In going over the same ground as Mr. Ellis, it is but natural that I should occasionally arrive at conclusions different from his, as, for instance, in the important question of the two *ee*s and *oo*s in Middle English, and in that of the preservation of short *y* in the Early Modern period.

But I have not been satisfied with merely summarizing and criticizing Mr. Ellis's views, but have also endeavoured to carry his method a step further, by combining his results with the deductions of the historical school inaugurated by Rask, and perfected by Grimm and his followers in Germany. Mr. Ellis's great achievement was to determine generally the phonetic values of the Roman alphabet in England at the different periods, and to establish the all-important principle that the Middle Age scribes wrote not by eye, but by ear, and consequently that their varying orthographic usage is a genuine criterion of their pronunciation. It has, therefore, been possible for me in the present essay to turn my attention more exclusively to the sounds themselves, and the wider generalizations obtainable from an examination of the various changes, which generalizations can again be applied to the elucidation and confirmation of the individual changes themselves. Many of the general principles stated at the beginning of the essay are, I believe, new and original; such, for instance, as the threefold divisions of sound-changes into organic, inorganic, and imitative, the sketch of the relations between sound and symbol (general alphabetics), the determination of the laws which govern the changes of short and long vowels in the Teutonic languages, etc.

I have also added to our stock of phonetic material, both by the observations on the pronunciation of Modern English and the living Teutonic languages, and also by the full lists of Old English words with their Middle and Modern equivalents, which afford a sound basis both for testing the views I have developed, and for carrying out further investigation.

It need hardly be said that the present essay is but a meagre sketch of what would be a really adequate history of English sounds. An investigation of every dialect and period, even if only on the meagre and imperfect scale here attempted, would fill many volumes. And yet till this is done, we cannot say that the foundations of a scientific English phonology are even laid. And it is only on such investigations that a satisfactory investigation of inflection and syntax can be based.

It was, therefore, absolutely necessary for me to limit my programme as much as possible. Hence the omission of any reference to our dialects, and the comparative neglect of the Middle period. Most of my results are obtained from a direct comparison with Old and Modern English: they are, therefore, to a certain extent, only tentative. In one point they are specially defective, namely as regards the deductions drawn from our present traditional orthography. Although this orthography is, on the whole, a very faithful representation of the pronunciation of the time when it settled into its present fixity, yet there are many of its details which urgently require a more minute examination. In short, we want a thorough investigation of the orthography of the sixteenth and seventeenth centuries, based on an examination not only of printed works, but also of manuscripts of all kinds. Such an investigation would not fail to yield valuable results.

Of the very considerable labour entailed in the present work, a large portion was expended on the lists. These I at first intended merely to consist of a certain number of examples of each change, but it proved so difficult to draw any definite line of exclusion that I determined to make them as full as possible, excluding only obsolete and doubtful words. There are a large number of words which, although of undoubted Teutonic origin, cannot be assigned to any Old English parent. Again, many Old English words given in the dictionaries without any reference, merely on the authority of Lye and Somner, are of very dubious existence. Many of them I believes to be gueses, formed by analogy from purely Modern words, while others are clearly taken from Transition texts. These I have often omitted, especially when they did not seem to offer any new points of interest. I am fully conscious of the inconsistencies and errors I have fallen into in preparing these lists, but I believe they are inevitable in a first attempt of this kind. It would have been easy to give my work a false appearance of fullness and finish, by suppressing the lists altogether; but I preferred to give them out, imperfect as they are, and rely on the indulgence of those who are alone competent to judge my work—those, namely, who have been engaged in similar initiatory investigations.

[*** Note also the tendency to lower *uu* before *r*, as shown in the almost universal *yòò*(*r*) for *yuur* (possessive of *yuu*). In the vulgar pronunciation this is carried out in all words, so that the combination *uur* is entirely lost. Thus we have *pòòə* for *puur*, *shòòə* for *shuur*, etc.]

PRINTED BY STEPHEN AUSTIN AND SONS, HERTFORD.

www.ingramcontent.com/pod-product-compliance
Lightning Source LLC
Chambersburg PA
CBHW022113160426
43197CB00009B/1001
* 9 7 8 3 3 3 7 1 2 5 3 3 2 *